SOLDIER ON:
My Rollercoster Ride From Range To Ring

Ross Burkinshaw

STEEL CITY PRESS

This first edition published in 2019 by Steel City Press
9 Ravenscroft Close, Sheffield, S13 8PN, United Kingdom.

ISBN 978-1-913047-06-1

With thanks to *Hayley Kirk Photography* for the photographs on the front cover,
and for numerous photographs throughout the book.

Proudly printed in the United Kingdom.

To my mum and dad

Thank you for always encouraging me, for always being there for me and believing in me. I'm so lucky to have had the opportunities that I've had.

To Glyn Rhodes, Ryan Rhodes, Kellie Maloney and Dennis Hobson

Thank you for being there for me at different stages of my career, and for giving me the opportunities to take part in some great fights.

To Paul 'Silky' Jones

Thank you for always being there and helping to guide me in the right direction from the very start.

To Frank Middleton

Thank you for always believing in me at every step of the way. You are deeply missed. May you rest in peace.

To 3 Rifles

Thank you for giving me the backing and support that you did, every step of the way.

To all my fans, friends and family

Thank you for following me up and down the country. It was a privilege to share that rollercoaster with you.

FOREWORD

By Herol 'Bomber' Graham

Ross had the talent and ability to become a world champion. I'm sure he would have made it to that level if it hadn't been for all his injuries.

I used to love training with Ross down at the gym. From a young age I could see that he was going to be a bright, good boxer. He had his own moves; looking at him, you just knew he had something special. He calls himself Ross the Boss, and Ross was always the Boss in his own way. He had power, especially in his weight categories.

Ross stood his ground. If you have an argument, you have an argument. If you have a disagreement, he respects you. But he'd always listen to you. He'd always be desperate to learn anything that he could. If you had something that he could learn from, he'd be there to listen. 'Can I do this? Can I do that?' He'd ask questions, and I'd give the answers. Sometimes I'd tell him that it was okay to just do it the way he already wanted to.

I've been through some tough times in my life. So has Ross. He's had to fight against all sorts of things. He's not had it easy either, there's things he's not really talked to anyone about until this book.

When you read this book, you'll see how much Ross values his mates. I can honestly say that Ross was a great lad, and a great mate. From skipping to sparring, he was the kind of person who'd light up the gym. We'd be messing around, teasing each other.

Ross was never afraid of a challenge. Even though I was a middleweight and he was a bantamweight at his heaviest, he'd still step into the ring and do some sparring with me. Ross wouldn't quit, or give up. He believed in his ability - and believe me, he had ability.

He was so fast, I'd find it difficult to hit him when we were sparring. I'm the Bomber, so I'd load up a few bombs for him but he'd get out of the way of most of them.

His style was a bit like mine, but I always used to say that he was more like a little Nas [Naseem Hamed]. He was just a damn good boxer: fast, and very adaptable.

Sometimes I think it's not fair to compare Ross to any other boxer. He did his own thing too. Once he knew what he was going to do, he never doubted himself.

I never doubted him either. Such a shame that he never got the chance to become a world champion. He really did deserve that shot. At the end of the day, don't compare him to anyone else. He was truly unique. He always did things his own way.

INDEX

Chapter 1

ROLLERCOASTER

It was the biggest day of my life in boxing so far. I'll never forget the date: May 30th, 2015 at the Magna Centre in Rotherham. I'd never wanted to box there. I'd been to a fight there some years before, supporting my mate Carl Wild, and just got a negative vibe about the place. Not tonight though: tonight was *my* night.

I was on a roll. I'd won the Commonwealth title, I'd won the European title. Only Klaas Mboyane stood between me and making it onto the world stage. The fight was for the WBO Intercontinental Bantamweight title, a stepping stone to a world title shot.

I was topping the bill in the biggest fight of my life so far, on the first boxing show ever to be aired in England on Spike TV. As I walked towards the ring I saw my mates Jake Grimstone and Ben Taylor, who'd followed every single one of my fights and spent money travelling all over the country to watch me. I *had* to win, to repay him and all my other fans for the confidence they'd shown in me over the years – supporting me through thick and thin.

I walked past my mates, head held high wearing my trademark Army beret. I always wore that beret coming in to the ring, because it reminded me of the pride I'd felt when I passed out to become a soldier. Wearing the beret was a way for me to focus on the things that mattered for a fighter: never giving in, fighting my corner whatever the odds.

Local songwriter Damon Hess had written a song specially for this fight, to use as my entrance music: 'Against All Odds'. "You can feel me, like a lightning bolt. You can hear me, like a thunder roar. Against all odds." As I walked past the VIP area, I could hear my mates cheering me on. The crowd was electric, the best I'd ever seen. Walking to the ring is the biggest adrenaline rush for a fighter, better than any drug.

Dennis Hobson, my manager, had chosen the matchup as one that I could win and allow him to manoeuvre me into a future world title fight. Ryan Rhodes, my trainer, had done the technical analysis. He'd told me that Mboyane was short, always coming forward and very tough. With my height and reach advantage, the plan was to stick to technical boxing. Stay behind my jab, with the occasional body shot to keep him off of me. I could gradually wear him down, then look for a finish towards the middle rounds of the fight – and if not, simply win on points. All that was needed was to execute the plan.

As I stepped into the ring, I immediately looked at Mboyane with a fighter's eyes. I was never one to watch too much footage of my opponents. It was my trainer's job to tell me how they fight, and mine to go into the ring and follow orders. I'm a military man at heart; following orders usually comes easy to me. Mboyane looked tough – very tough – but much smaller than me. Ryan was absolutely spot on as ever.

From that point on, nothing else mattered. I could see my family at ringside, but this was the moment to focus. All I could think about was the fight; gradually everything else zoned out as I got to the point of supreme clarity. I kept my eyes fixed straight on Mboyane, thinking 'I'm gonna 'ave you. I can take you'.

Even though everyone was shouting, I would just pick out the voices of those most important to me. I'd hear a snippet from my wife Nicola, or from Ryan, or even at that time from Dennis. Then there's that tiny moment, when it feels as though all the noise of the crowd goes silent – just for a second. We touch gloves and the entire arena waits, looking forward to the first bell and the action beginning. That moment is electric. Even now, writing this, the hair on the back of my neck is standing up and my heart is pounding just thinking back to it. I love to entertain people; I love being centre stage: headlining a show, live on television on a channel that everyone could watch for free – I felt king of the whole world that night.

The bell sounded for the start of the first round, and it was time to get to work.

I came out confidently, staying behind my jab as instructed. With my reach advantage, I tried to throw longer hook shots to keep him at bay. Mboyane was a seasoned fighter who knew what he was doing, so the fight wasn't going to be completely lop-sided but it was clear that the pre-fight plan was going to prove effective. Unlike my 'war' with Jason Cunningham for the Commonwealth title, this one should have been fairly comfortable: not exactly a walk in the park, but a brisk jog. Every now and then, he would come forward throwing body shots and catch me with something – but there can't have been a person watching it outside of Mboyane's personal camp who didn't think that I bossed Round 1. Of course I bossed it; I'm not known as Ross the Boss for nothing.

The bell rang, and Round 1 was over. Ryan was quick to offer advice, the advice I needed to hear. "Keep doing what you're doing. Stick to your boxing, and don't get involved in no wars."

Ryan always said to me that the best thing that he could do would be to 'take my balls away', because I always fought with my heart and not my head. Nothing had dented my confidence at all; in some ways I'm my own worst enemy. I'm not ashamed to admit that I struggle with depression on a daily basis. Because I try to take such a positive approach to life, I was never really able to admit it to myself. It's not the Army way either: whatever the trouble, you get on and make sure that you get through it.

I was in many ways a confidence fighter; when I was truly in that zone I was absolutely unstoppable. If I could only defeat my biggest opponent, then I could quite literally beat the world.

In Round 2, Mboyane came out fighting. He knew that he'd lost the first round, and was determined to make an impact in the second. He was trying to turn the fight into a war, knowing that with my superior reach he wouldn't be able to beat me by boxing skills alone. He'd probably studied footage of me, seen my

Cunningham fight, and expected my style to be more bruising, going toe to toe. He would have been happy with that, and tried to force me into doing the same.

I found myself having to fight against the urge to allow him to do it: if there's one thing I loved, it was a good scrap. There was only one thing I wanted more, and that was to become a world champion – so I had to follow Ryan's orders. It was instinct versus head, and my head was winning but I can't honestly say that there weren't a few exchanges where I was roughing it up in my old style.

Ryan's advice in my corner at the end of the round was consistent: don't get drawn into the wrong style of fight. It was sensible and correct. I was pretty confident that I had two rounds in the bag, and was well on my way to victory. In Round 3, though, a single punch transformed the fight. Mboyane threw a right hook to the body. I saw it coming and tucked up. His hook missed, but inadvertently caught my left elbow. My whole life suddenly changed, with that one punch.

Just over a week before the fight, my last spar was against Paul Butler, former World Champion, at Anthony Farnell's gym in Manchester. Butler was known for his powerful body shots; after the spar, Butler's dad came up to me – impressed – and said that I was going to stop Mboyane with a body shot.

During the sparring, we'd inadvertently come together and I'd chipped a bone in that elbow. It had been touch and go whether I'd even make the Mboyane fight, but I decided to go ahead. I couldn't let my fans down, and I wasn't going to let a little thing like a chipped bone stop me. I always used to joke to others when they were injured that they should 'man up and get some Calpol down them'. I wasn't going to pull out of this fight because of something as minor as that; it'd be as bad as blaming a poorly toe for a defeat.

As we walked out of the gym, Ryan said to me "Well done. After a performance like that, we'll finish on a high. That's your last spar." The way my elbow reacted, I don't think I'd have been capable of sparring again anyway.

So when Mboyane's hook caught the same elbow, it suddenly erupted in agony. I knew instantly that something was deeply wrong, and from that moment it became almost impossible for me to throw my left hand. The problem was, my left is my jabbing hand. To keep control of a fight, to keep my opponent at bay, I needed to be able to throw the jab as a high-volume punch. If you've got a reach advantage in a fight, your first name should be 'jab', your middle name should be 'jab', and your surname should be 'jab'. It's not rocket science, you just hit them whilst they're in your reach but you're out of theirs.

I got back to my corner, but having been unable to really snap out my jab later in the round, it became a little more touch and go. Hand on heart, I don't know if I won the third round or not. Some will have given it to one fighter or the other; perhaps it should have been scored as a level round. Ryan was shouting at me to throw the jab more, and I'd had to tell him about the injury.

In Round 4, I pretty much couldn't throw my left at all. It's so frustrating, being in a fight with tens of thousands of people across the country watching, without being able to throw the most basic punch in boxing. Everyone could see that there was something wrong: the commentators had been criticising me for my tactics in Round 3, but by Round 4 they twigged that there was an injury.

I got back to the corner, telling Ryan "My arm's fucking killing me". Dennis Hobson had noticed there was something wrong, and came over to ask what was up. I said "My elbow's killing". Dennis was pretty straightforward. Up to this fight, he'd always looked out for me. "Pull him out. If you pull him out now, he'll be able to fight another day." If it had been in the eleventh or twelfth round, I might have been able to survive till the final bell and hope that I could win on the judges' scorecards. Perhaps I could have survived another round or two going southpaw, and jabbing with my right hand instead. After just four rounds though, there was no way that I could realistically continue – much less win the fight.

They went to tell the referee that I needed to pull out, saying "His shoulder's gone." I tried to protest that it was my elbow, not my shoulder, and was told in no uncertain terms that I had to 'shut up'. Because of that, the commentators on TV told everyone that it was a shoulder injury but it wasn't. I don't know why they said that it was my shoulder but ironically, a few months later when sparring with Gavin McDonnell and preparing for my comeback fight, I popped my shoulder out. I retired without ever getting back into the ring.

Chapter 2

BOSS BABY

If you're wanting one of those boxing stories about a young boy fighting against a troubled family background, turmoil at home and all that, you've come to the wrong place. My dad was a joiner; my mum taught decoupage at Stocksbridge college. I'm just a working-class lad from Stocksbridge, the kind you'd find on the terraces any given Saturday afternoon, singing my heart out for Sheffield Wednesday. My parents worked hard for a living, always taking care of me and my sister.

The worst you can say about my early years is that I got into a few fights. Actually, if I'm honest, I got into a *lot* of fights at school. That's the thing about young kids who are going to grow up to be bantamweights: they're really small, a bit skinny, and an easy target for bullies. I wasn't going to be an easy target for anyone; I had something they didn't - determination, and the desire to win no matter the odds.

I never looked for trouble. I was never the person to start a fight, but I made absolutely certain that I was the one to finish it. I stand by that to this day. My dad knew the score, so he started taking me to ju-jitsu classes. Don't get me wrong, ju-jitsu was okay - but there wasn't enough punching. I loved the sparring at the end of each session, so my dad started to look for something more. At the age of 8, he took me to what used to be Hillsborough Boys'

Club - where Ray Gillott used to run a boxing gym. There was a poster on the wall advertising one of Clinton Woods' fights, and another for Paul 'Silky' Jones, boxing for the world title against Verno Phillips. I remember thinking 'I wanna be like them when I'm older', and that was it. The moment I put on the gloves, I just knew that this was going to be my life.

Ray Gillot with Ross, 1995

I'm going to give Ray Gillott so much credit, not just for being a great first trainer and teaching me the basics of boxing, but because he's somebody who has just so much passion for the sport and for the people. Even now, when I train white-collar fighters to raise money for charity, Ray comes down - in his 70s - and helps out. That's the thing about boxing, at least outside the stage-managed spotlight of world title fights and manufactured grudge matches: it's more like a family than just making friends. You look out for each other. You make a friend, and they're your friend for life.

I was in my element, learning to bob and weave, duck and dive, throw my jab and catch my opponent. I was never afraid to take a shot to land one; that's the true brawler in me. It's all about self-confidence. If I know I can punch harder than my opponent, and if I know I can take a punch better than he can, then I'm going to win. It's as simple as that.

Fighting at school was never too far away, and I got myself expelled from junior school after being involved in one fight too many. On my first day at the new school, a lad called Tom Hind came up to me:

"Are you Ross Burkinshaw?"

"Yes, why?"

"Did you get expelled for fighting at your last school?"

"Yeah"

Bang! He punched me right in the face. I didn't have time to hit him back right there and then. Schools have the habit of expecting you to turn up to classes when the bell goes. But at the end of the day, I stood outside the school gates waiting for him. He'd started the fight, so I didn't back down. I did what I always do. I finished it.

If you've never been involved in boxing, you might think I'd just made an enemy for life. In fact, it was quite the opposite. I never really lost touch with him even decades later, and one day he came into my gym. I gave him some basic training, and he fought on one of my recent white-collar boxing bills at the New York Stadium in Rotherham. He still comes down to the gym on a Wednesday night, regular as clockwork, keeping in shape. It wasn't the only time that's happened either. Craig Smith was a good mate, but when I was at school it seemed that my mum and dad were called in every other week about me fighting with him. He was into fishing, and he had this massive landing net. He tied me up and was going to drag me into the River Don. I managed to get my way out, but I never backed down. The next day, I went down with my other mate and settled the score.

That's just who I am. I can forgive you for punching me in the face, no problem, but I take people as I find them. Got a problem with me? Tell me to my face. Don't go around, behind my back, moaning and whining, complaining and stirring up trouble. If you've got a problem with me, I can deal with that and we can sort things. I just hate the whole 'I'm supposed to hate this person because my mate once fell out with their mate' thing. Life's too short for that. Sort things out over a pint, or in the boxing ring if you must, but just be yourself and be honest.

I was waiting far too long for my first proper fight though. They'd brought in an age limit for amateur boxing. The age limit for competing had previously been reduced from 11 to 10, so I thought I was going to get my first match quicker than expected. I was buzzing as I waited for my tenth birthday. But then when I turned 10, apparently I wasn't heavy enough to get a fight. My first fight got delayed again for that reason. Then by the time I was heavy enough, the rules had changed again. Now you had to be 11 to be allowed to compete.

Worse still, I had a problem with the gym. We found out that my gym was threatened with closing down, so I decided to do a sponsored run to raise money. I even managed to get in touch with Paul Silky Jones, and fair play to him, he helped me no end. Says a lot about a world champion boxer, that he was prepared to talk to and help a young kid like me whilst still fighting at the top of his game. He even took me on the pads, which was such a huge boost!

Paul Silky Jones with Ross. 1996

This is why I say that boxing is so much like a family. When I won my first belt (the English title), Silky was the first one to phone me to congratulate me. He said I'm now in a new club, with the elite champions.

Sponsored run. 1996

I managed to raise £675, which was a lot of money for a kid in those days, but we weren't able to keep Ray's gym from closing, so we donated the money to Sheffield Children's Hospital. At least it went to a good cause, but I had no gym to train at. I went down to Brendan Ingle's gym one Saturday with my grandad, Brian. I can't speak highly enough of Brendan as a human being, rest in peace pal, because he revolutionised British boxing. At that time, anyone who trained four world champions, six European, fifteen British and six Commonwealth champions was likely to do that. It's not like today, when it seems that every time you blink there's another British boxer getting a world title. Seriously, twenty years ago it'd have been a major event for a British lad to get a world title shot. These days, sometimes it happens and you barely even notice. That's the quality and strength in depth of our boxing today.

But somehow, Brendan's style wasn't quite suited to me, or perhaps my style wasn't suited to him, probably because I was so direct in my approach. I don't think 'take one to land one' was really what he was looking for in a fighter somehow.

Instead, Paul 'Silky' Jones (who'd even met up with us on the sponsored run) came up trumps: he suggested that I should go down to Sheffield Boxing Centre and Glyn Rhodes. I found myself being trained by Frank Middleton. He knew Ray Gillott, and through my connection, Ray eventually ended up coming down and training me there. They all knew their stuff, but I still hadn't had a fight. After over a year of waiting - and believe me, when you're 10 or 11 years old, waiting over a year feels like a lifetime - finally I got the chance to step into the ring and show what I could do. I can still remember my first fight (well, the first fight wearing gloves, let's put it that way): it was on the 23rd of October 1997, at the Manor Social Club.

First fight. 1997

Paul Silky Jones even let me have one of his robes that he'd used to enter the ring for a World Title fight. That was a huge boost to my confidence, for my first ever amateur fight walking out in a world champion's robe. He let me keep it too, though I eventually gave it back to him in 2017.

I'd like to tell you all about that fight, but I can't. The bell rang, and I started punching. Even the 90-second rounds seemed to last an eternity. It's all a blur though, my first fight and all that adrenaline coursing through my veins. All I know is that I won, because that's what I'm determined to do every single time I fight - whether that's a physical fight or any other kind of struggle. I back myself to win every time. If you don't know me, you might think it's arrogance - but it's not. But then again, if you really know me, you know it is. If you don't believe in yourself, how will you ever truly succeed?

I was never very good at football, but team sports didn't interest me so much for that reason. If your team wins or loses at football, it's a team effort. Even if you put in a man-of-the-match performance, it's entirely possible that you could still lose. In boxing, there are no excuses (apart from David Haye's toe and Amir Khan's low blow from Crawford). There's nobody else to blame but yourself if you mess up, and you have to back yourself 100% to succeed. The boxing ring can be a very lonely place if you don't have confidence, and if there's one thing I wasn't lacking, it was self-confidence. It's a strange mix, isn't it? My struggles with depression have made the newspapers, but stick some 8oz gloves on my fists and I'll deliver. You wouldn't ask a gardener to fix your electrics, but I bet he'd know what to do with your garden.

Put me inside the square ring, and something just changes inside my brain.

One thing that never changes, though, is the feeling when you step into the ring. It was exactly the same at 11 years old as it was the last time I boxed as a professional. On the rare occasions when I wasn't nervous, I didn't perform so well. I needed that nervousness, the energy and adrenaline, to spur me on to succeed. So much changed from child to adult, but that feeling of anticipation never leaves. Since I retired, I miss it so much.

It was always difficult for them to match me with opponents, just because I was naturally very light. I suppose there aren't that many people of my build who take up boxing when they're as young as I was. But Frank Middleton and my matchmaker Harry Cliff had a solution, one that Brendan Ingle also used with a young Naseem Hamed. In the professional ranks, boxers often have to work very hard to keep their weight down. I had to do the opposite - to look like I weighed more than I actually did. Frank would put lead weights inside my shoes, so I'd appear heavier on the scales and be allowed to fight. My dad made those weights, wrapped in gaffer tape so they went inside my socks and nobody could see them.

It was actually great practice for my later professional boxing career. Think about it: I got used to fighting people heavier than me, people who packed a punch. When you're not scared of fighting someone bigger, it stands you in great stead for anything you might meet later in your career. You're just not going to be particularly fazed by it. I just had to learn to punch harder. It was the same as a professional; I always liked to spar with bigger and heavier opponents. If I could cope with their punches, nothing I met on fight night was ever going to surprise me. People always used to tell me that I punched well above my weight, or that I had 'heavy hands'. Opponents respected my power, but that power comes from hard work and good technique. I learned lots of that as a young boxer from Herol 'Bomber' Graham. He's always had my back, and I'm proud that he agreed to do the foreword for this book. Having him do the foreword, and Silky on the back cover, is a great reminder of the big names who have always been there for me.

Back at school, you might think that other kids would have stopped starting fights with me - but actually, the opposite happened. They knew that I was a boxer, so the lads who fancied themselves as being 'big', 'tough' and 'hard' would always want to prove it by trying to beat me up. Like I said, I've been fighting all my life. It was better, though, to do my talking in the ring. I owe so much to boxing, because it gave me something to focus on. From the moment I stepped into Ray's gym at the age of 8, I knew what I wanted to be when I grew up: a professional boxer.

It didn't really stop. When I was 15, I went on holiday to Cuba just before my GCSEs. My dad went up to the school and asked if it was okay to take me out for a once-in-a-lifetime holiday. They said yes, which I guess wouldn't have been allowed today, but it was an amazing chance.

On the last night, my dad got into some trouble in the bar with some Germans. One of them, a proper 6 foot 3 bruising-looking bloke, was getting ready to punch my dad. I wasn't going to have that, so I went up and landed one right on his nose. He had to go to hospital, and wasn't allowed to fly home the next day. Even at that age, I wasn't going to let anyone get away with threatening my family.

My teachers used to tell me to knuckle down and get some work done. These days, it's more likely to be Claire who works alongside me, or my publisher or my accountant trying to get me to focus on the boring administration that needs doing. We've been working on this book for over a year, but trying to tie me down to get it finished is hard work for anyone. It's still the same problem though. It's easier to focus on practical stuff than admin.

Back then, I'd have rather been in the gym preparing for a fight than sitting in school. Today, I'd rather be in the gym training people than sitting around at home doing the paperwork, shuffling my credit cards and paying the bills.

They always used to tell me that everyone has a dream, and that academic work was important in case my dream didn't quite come true. I was determined to make my dreams come true, and sometimes the price you pay for such single-mindedness is that you don't achieve as much as you should at school.

When I was a kid, I used to find any excuse to wag off school. I'd go and knock on the door of John Wainright (Wainy) and my other mates Harris, Kango and Taylor, and my best mate Tony Button and we'd go down Ewden reservoir and poach some trout. Sometimes Craig Smith would come down with us. Being a total

Del Boy, I knew where the overflow bit was where all the trout would gather. It was so easy to catch them, using tin foil or bread on the end of the hook. I was the master at splodging. We'd then sell the trout on and make a bit of cash.

One day, my mate's mum and dad Jackie and Glyn were off work and walking the dogs. I told them what we were doing, and they ended up ordering five trout off me. I got them home, skinned them, gutted them and everything, and got them back to their house ready for tea. That mate married my sister Carla just a couple of weeks ago. I flew out to Mexico to see them get married. Carla's just like me, she has to do everything spectacularly. My mate is now now my brother-in-law. They say you can choose your friends but you can't choose your family, but I'm glad that my friend has become family.

In time, though, when I was at secondary school my teachers started to collect the clippings from the newspapers to follow my development as an amateur boxer. Slowly, they started to realise that my pipe dreams were actually worth fighting for. I was going places, but don't be under any illusions that the world of professional boxing is easy or even always as glamorous as you see when Anthony Joshua or Tyson Fury takes to the ring in front of a sold-out stadium.

Every injury, every cancelled fight, every defeat, every argument with a trainer or promoter - they can all do serious damage to your career and mind. And when you've focused so much on that, giving up so much else, you're on your own.

Sometimes, it wasn't just Ross Burkinshaw against whichever faceless opponent was standing in the blue corner.

Sometimes, it was Ross Burkinshaw against the world.

Chapter 3

INTO THE LIMELIGHT

"You're never too important to be nice to people"

If there's one thing that training with Glyn did for me, it opened my eyes to what boxing was like at the top level. When I was about 12, I used to walk into the ring and carry the British, Commonwealth and European belts in for Clinton Woods. That was before he won his world belt.

Carrying Clinton's belts, 1999

I remember one time, me and Carl Wild heard one of the guys in the gym saying he was going down to London for one of Woods' fights. We blagged a lift from him down to London, phoned our parents and told them we were going. That's just how it was. They trusted us. When we got down there, I used a phone box to ring Dennis and got myself into the venue to carry Clinton's belts. A little thing, but I got used to the big-fight atmosphere. That would help me later in life, because I'd become so comfortable with being in that kind of arena.

As a teenager, I got the chance to meet so many boxing idols. For a couple of his fights, after parting ways with Brendan Ingle, Prince Naseem Hamed - possibly Sheffield's most famous boxer ever - trained at Glyn's gym. Actually, he rented a room just behind the main gym so that he could train privately without being distracted by everyone else in the gym.

'Leopard print' shorts

A lot of people knock Nas, but I can only tell it as I saw it. He was an absolutely top-notch fighter, and he was amazing, better than you could possibly expect any fighter to be towards a young kid trying to develop his own way. Although nobody else was allowed in to the private training room, Nas always allowed me to go back - and even to train with him at times. Where do you think my silky skills, bobbing and weaving, come from? One day, Adidas came up to do a photoshoot with

Nas. He even asked me to take part in the photoshoot. He had me shadow-boxing, he took me on the pads, and he told everyone who was there that I could hit harder than he did at that age. The impact that had on me, as a young teen desperate to make it in boxing, was incredible. He even once had a pair of shorts made for me with his own trademark 'leopard print' material.

He really looked after me, and I don't just mean with advice and words - he backed it up too. Nas used to get me, my mum and dad passes to fights, and his brother Nabeel started to sponsor me too. I remember being invited to his fight against Vuyani Bungu in March 2000, which took place at London Olympia. Nas was talking to me whilst warming up. These two guys walked in, just as Naseem's brothers had to leave. "Can you talk to Sean for me?" they asked. Turned out that 'Sean' was Sean John Combs, better known as Puff Daddy.

Nas got into the ring and did his thing. In the fourth round, the American commentators on HBO were busy asking why Naseem Hamed hadn't knocked anyone out recently. Their discussion was interrupted by a thunderous left-hand hammer blow from Nas, stopping Bungu with that one punch. Bungu might just about have beaten the count, but he was in no position to continue. Nas certainly proved them wrong that day, and I always loved proving my own critics wrong too. That night was the first time in my life that I'd ever been shy, and I missed out as a result. The guy who was with Puff Daddy, who I think was Mase, said "Put him on your shoulders". I don't know why, but I got shy and said no. If I hadn't suddenly developed that uncharacteristic shyness, I would have been pictured in every newspaper. I still love the publicity, even now. Nothing ever changes.

We went back into the changing rooms, and there were people everywhere congratulating Nas. I found myself talking to Ronnie Wood from the Rolling Stones. At that point, meeting so many heroes and idols, I remember thinking 'I definitely want this life when I get older'.

In June of the next year, Glyn Rhodes and Matt Mowat (another professional trainer, who would often be my cornerman in later years when I turned professional) planned a gym trip to New York, to the international boxing Hall of Fame in Canastota. There weren't so many kids from the gym who were able to go, but I did - helped out, partly, by Naseem's brother Nabeel. At the time it was just meant to be a trip to the Hall of Fame, but by the time we were finished, it ended up being so much more than that. I always used to have my head shaved when I was a kid, but my mum didn't like it. She thought it looked a bit scruffy. I

Boxing Hall of Fame, 2001

needed some spending money when I went to New York, so she paid me £100 to grow my hair. After I came back, I decided I actually liked it that way.

But I wasn't going to tell me mam that - whenever I got a bit short of cash, I'd just tell her I was going to shave my head and suddenly the 'bank of mum and dad' was open for business.

It just so happened that we were in New York on June 8th, 2001. That date was the first time in history that a pay-per-view boxing event had ever been headlined by women fighters. Laila Ali, daughter of Muhammad Ali, was due to fight Jacqui Frazier-Lyde, daughter of Joe Frazier. The rivalry between Muhammad Ali and Joe Frazier was perhaps the greatest in the history of boxing, with the 'Fight of the Century' and 'Thrilla in Manilla' being two of their three meetings.

When their daughters, both unbeaten in their own careers so far, came face-to-face in the boxing ring, an eager American press dubbed it as 'Frazier-Ali IV'.

We checked in to our New York hotel in the early hours of the morning. The next day, we walked out of the hotel room - and Laila Ali just happened to be staying in the room just two rooms along from us. We got talking to her in the lift, and asked if her dad was going to watch the fight. The answer was no; he never came to see any of her fights.

On the plane on the way over, I'd been reading a book: Muhammad Ali - More than a Hero, by Laila's sister Hana Ali. I explained this to Laila. She told me to get the book and to wait in the hotel lobby. Sure enough, she got her sister to come over to meet me and sign the book. It was just another story of the 'boxing family'.

Ross with Laila Ali

People say boxing's a brutal sport, and in a way it is, but there's such human compassion and kindness all the way through the sport at every level. It just fills me with horror, whenever I hear people clamouring for boxing to be banned. Just imagine if all those lives that have been changed through boxing could never have been changed. I wonder sometimes what I'd have done with my life, if they weren't there.

The fight took place at the Turning Stone Casino in Verona, New York. I was sitting with Glyn and Matt on fight night, when I spotted that Sugar Ray Leonard was at ringside. I thought I had to at least get his autograph or something, so I asked the security guards - who I remember looked more like Canadian mounties than security - to let me through. They said no, but I was still very small for my age. When they turned away and started chatting, I slipped through and found Sugar Ray Leonard. He let me sit next to him and chatted for about half an hour. Glyn and Matt had shaved off one of my eyebrows as a prank, so I looked quite odd - but it worked out well because it helped me to get Sugar Ray Leonard's attention! The promoter Don King was there too, though I didn't really get a chance to speak to him at that moment.

The next day, we'd got tickets to an evening billed as the 'banquet of champions'. There were all kinds of big names sitting at the top table: Leon Spinks (who'd once beaten Muhammed Ali), Angelo Dundee (Ali's trainer), Ken Norton (who boxed Ali and Foreman, and was once billeted to play Apollo Creed in the Rocky films), Michael Spinks (whose only defeat was to Mike Tyson)…there were a lot of big names at that table. So I did my thing, and walked up to the table to get a photo. Once again, they weren't going to let me through - but Don King recognised me from the fight the night before and said "Let the kid from England through. If the boy wants a photo, he can have one." I told him that I'd be a professional myself one day and that I was going to become a champion. I suppose he must have heard that from hundreds of kids over the years, but when I said it, I meant it. I made it happen. Later, back at the hotel, I also got myself a picture with Felix Tito Trinidad. WBA, WBC, IBF…the welterweight champion had won world titles with the various different boards of control.

Some day, I thought, it's going to be the other way around. People are going to want to get their pictures taken with me. I didn't want to bask in reflected glory from them; I wanted to make my own name for myself. If it hadn't been for that shoulder injury, I'd have had a world title belt of my own. I'm absolutely convinced of that. Still, the Commonwealth and European titles were a great achievement.

We flew back from JFK airport on June 11th, 2001 - three months to the day before the terror attacks on 9/11. It really brought home to me just how precious and fragile life is, and how what matters isn't just picking up autographs from famous people. Family matters so much. Family means so many different things. There's the family you're born into, there's the family you chose by getting married, and then there's the boxing family.

Thinking back now, I wonder whether flying out of New York so close to 9/11 played a part in my decision to join the Army. One way or another, just a couple of months after coming back from the trip, it really put my life and priorities into perspective.

Chapter 4

SAVING PRIVATE BURKINSHAW

From leaving school, my GCSE results were never going to be that good. I'd never really focused on academic work, because I'd always had my heart set on one thing: that I was going to be a professional boxer. That wasn't something I could go into straight away at the age of 16, coming out of school. I needed to be able to develop my strength first. I walked straight into a job as a joiner, following the 'family business', just like my dad when he'd left school. I already knew how to do it because in my last year, I'd been wagging school to go and do some work as a joiner, working cash-in-hand for a friend.

It was just a job to me though, and I was looking for something more. After a few months of doing a joinery apprenticeship at Castle College on a day release scheme, where I honestly spent more time with Lee Crooks and our mates drinking WKD Blue rather than learning dovetail joints, I went out to Canada on holiday. I got it into my head that I was going to move out there, and quit my job to move. I'm not sure my heart was really in that move, though, because I didn't put all the effort in to make it happen. Sitting around, unemployed, at the age of 16, meant I was always going to get a certain amount of pressure from my mum and dad to do something. Anything.

I didn't really feel like I'd got much direction in life. Not many kids of age 16 are ready to become professional boxers, and in any case you weren't allowed to turn professional until the age of 18, but what do you do in the meantime? Lots of things started to push me towards joining the Army. I'd always been proud of my country, and believed that I should be prepared to fight for it. Fighting, after all, was my business in so many ways. That memory, flying back from New York exactly three months before 9/11, kept coming back to me. Then, whilst my mum and dad had gone away on holiday, I'd have the television on and I'd be watching the news about our troops over in Iraq.

I started to read Nigel Benn's autobiography - The Dark Destroyer. He talked about the Army boxing team, about how they had the best life and how the Army really looked after their boxers. My mum in particular was constantly on at me to get a new job. I said to her that I'm "gonna join the Army and I'm gonna box in the Army". I kept thinking that I wanted to get out there. Mum said "alright then, go and do it". She definitely gave me the impression that she believed I wouldn't actually go through with it, but I'm the kind of guy who likes to prove everyone wrong. Even now, all anyone has to say is 'You can't do this' or 'I dare you to do that' and I'll do it, no matter how crazy or ridiculous it seems.

My dad took me down to see the Army careers people. If you haven't yet twigged, I'm a very impulsive kind of person. I'm impulsive in a very strange sort of way though. I'll make major decisions instantly based on a gut feeling or instinct, but then worry about minor ones. That might mean 30 minutes sitting and staring at a menu trying to decide what I want to eat, but when I was with Nicola I'd go out and buy a new car without checking with her first. I really need to stop doing that.

We met Simon Barker of the Light Infantry on the desk upstairs. I said that I want to box and to be in the army. He said that the First Battalion was the best for boxing in the whole of the Army. Recruiters will tell you anything to get you to sign on the dotted line. So naturally I wanted to sign up there and then. When I'm determined to do something, I make it happen in one way or another. When someone told me that I couldn't turn professional as a boxer whilst still a serving soldier in the Army, I went ahead and got the rules changed.

My dad asked me "Are you sure that you wanna do this?", and I was. If you were under 16 & 9 months at that time, you'd have to sign up as a junior entry. I didn't want to do that because that meant a longer training period before getting to the battalion. Luckily, I hit that milestone on August 10th - so I joined on August 12th as an adult entry. I said goodbye to me mum and dad, then headed off to join the Army. I got on the train up to Darlington, then met the Army's coach to take me down to Catterick. I was 'shitting mi' sen'; I was the youngest and smallest one there. Some of the other recruits were as old as 28. We were standing outside the station, queuing up, and a big white coach pulled up. Corporal Gaghan (nicknamed Giggsy after Ryan Giggs) got off and ordered us "Right, get in line!"

I thought "Fuck, here we go. Shit's just got real." It had, indeed, got real. I was no longer Ross Burkinshaw. Now, I was "25168854

Private Burkinshaw, SIR!" - and identified myself as such for the next six months. I'd made it to the ITC (Infantry Training Centre) Catterick. I was to be in 3 Platoon, Korea Company.

We got into our room, which I can still picture now. We were ordered to dump our stuff, stand by our beds, and wait. Quietly. At least I'd got a lad called Kev Hall in my room, who I'd done my infantry selection with up at Glencorse Barracks in Scotland. At least I felt like I had a mate straight away, and it helped that he was a lot older than me, more mature, and able to look after me a bit. He certainly did. When I re-read that paragraph, the memory flooded back to me so overwhelmingly that I can remember it like it was yesterday. That same overpowering smell came straight back.

Everyone was known by their surnames. We had Drake (Tom, nickname Drakey), Underwood (Dennis, nickname Denzil - 'cos nobody could spell Denzel), Asamoah-junior (Atta), and the friendliest warrior that I've ever met, Kokahu from Tonga. I had so much respect for this guy, he was so nice and so tough as well. Then there was Starkey (Aidan). He turned out to be a really good lad, though at first some of the lads described him as 'camp as Christmas'. There were a couple of others as well who I've lost touch with over the years.

We just waited, for what was probably only a few minutes or half an hour but seemed like a week. We started whispering to each other to get to know each other a little better, like a bunch of kids on an overnight school trip. It felt just like a fight: I was nervous and excited, or - as I liked to put it - "my arse was going from 50p to 5p wondering what the fuck I was doing".

We had to come in, fill in some forms, fill out some forms, have some injections, and get a squaddie short, back and sides haircut - if we had hair. Some of the 27 and 28 year olds were going bald already. My short, back and sides haircut is still there today; I thought of that when I had my haircut earlier. This was back in the days before political correctness managed to find its way into the Army. Caught talking, they'd clip you round the ear. I'm not going to mention the names of the corporals that did it, but they ended up being my friends.

Ross and the lads. 2003

After a couple of months, I was starting to settle in a bit. One night, one of the guys from next door - Adam Oumchief (I hope I've got the spelling right) was in our room. Giggsy came back, shall we say, a little pissed up. For a change. He trashed all the lockers in the room. I stood up out of bed. He responded by asking me what I thought I was doing, and stubbed a cigarette out on my arm. I've still got the scar to prove it now. Then, he said "you think you're right hard, I bet Oumchief could take you". I didn't like people making out that 'cos I was small they could have done me.

For some reason, when I disagreed, Oumchief took offence at this. We ended up fighting in the room, with the door closed, with the corporal there. Oumchief was maybe 26 or 27, and I'm not sure I'd even turned 17. It turned into a full-blown fight. He wasn't backing down; he pulled his penknife out. Part of the frame of the door was broken. I pulled that out, and the frame came out in my hand with nails still stuck in. Now we each had a weapon.

Drunk or not, that's the point at which Giggsy remembered the stripes on his arm and that things could have gotten a little out of hand. The referee waved the fight off, with what I think was the first and only technical-draw decision of my career.

Ever desperate to make money, it wasn't long before Del Boy was back in action. At the time, I didn't really drink or smoke. Everyone else did, and their wage packets were usually spent on cigarettes and alcohol faster than I could throw an uppercut-hook-backhand-hook combination. So naturally they'd ask to borrow money off other people. We used to call it 'double bubble money', interest rates more comparable to Wonga than a mortgage. Lend them £20, and they give you £40 back when they next got paid. That business model worked well for me. I managed to find £200 to lend out, and got £400 back on payday. Soon, word had spread that loan-shark lender Ross was in town. I maybe lent out £400 in the second month and got back £800.

By the third month, the corporals had found out that I was doing it. Everyone was asking to borrow money from me, but my wage packet was only £930 per month. I just didn't have enough to lend out. Now, the corporals got in on the action. They gave me the additional money to lend out, double their own money, and I'd make a few drinks out of each transaction.

I could have put that money in the bank, but being a young teenager with cash, I spent it. I always do. We might go to Richmond, spending a day sightseeing. Instead of catching the bus, we'd take taxis and stuff like that. I always had to have the best TV, and was kept buying clothes to look my best - if I had money, I didn't keep it for very long.

When we went out on exercise, everyone would live on ration packs. The corporals would shout for me, as though I was in trouble. I had to commando-crawl across the harbour area to the corporals. They'd take me around the back. Everyone'd be thinking 'What's Burky done now?' They'd be shouting 'Burkinshaw, get here!'. I'd get to my corporals, and boom! There was the full McDonalds, quarter-pounder with cheese meal (no sauce, just the way I like it) sat waiting for me whilst everyone else was sat back scoffing their ration packs. Sometimes, that was my payment for helping them to double their money.

The last week of training, the Korea Company Sergeant-Major

called me to the office and sat me down. I'd been busted. "You've been double-bubbling money haven't you, Burkinshaw?"

"No Sir!"

"You have, we know the corporals have been helping you out."

"They haven't, sir. I'll tell you the truth. I've lent a few quid out but no-one's ever helped me. I wish they did. I did it mi'sen."

Little did I know at the time that there was someone outside the office listening. The interview ended, and I walked out. One of the corporals was stood at the end of corridor. He looked me in the eye and winked.

The next day, I passed out of basic training and went home.

Chapter 5

BECOMING THE BOSS

"Believe and achieve"

Two weeks later, I flew to Cyprus where the second battalion light infantry was based. I'd switched from the first battalion to the second, because the first battalion boxing team wasn't going at the time as they'd just got back from Iraq. So much for the idea that the first battalion had the best boxing team in the Army. Unless they'd been donning gloves to search for Saddam, someone had clearly been telling me a few porkies.

Ross back at the battalion when boxing professionally

On the first night, I got to the battalion headquarters. I woke up with a hangover the next day, having learned by this time the delights of copious quantities of alcohol and the impact it has on the body when you're only a tad over 8 stone. We were given our induction to battalion life, sitting down doing our induction cadre under a red-hot blazing sun, when this lad walked over.

"Who's Burky?" The lad had clearly been in the regiment for some time. We all looked at each other.

"Me, Sir", I replied.

"I'm not a Sir, I work for a living", he said in true Army fashion. Anyone who wasn't a commissioned officer described themselves in that way. There were the officers, and there were the soldiers who actually did the work.

I should probably point out before we go much further that I'm not being totally eccentric when I flip between Sergeant and Serjeant on a regular basis. There is a reason: it's only Sergeant in the rest of the Army. The Light Division was at the time the only division to stick to using the traditional j spelling.

He called me to go round the back, then once out of earshot, he said:
"I've had a phone call, me. We know you didn't grass about your double bubbling. Davver says you're a good egg. You'll be looked after here."

That night, I found out that - like Lannisters - a Corporal of the Second Light Infantry always pays his debts. The first night there, the horrors and carnage of an initiation for new recruits were in full swing. There were people getting hung off the balcony in their doss-bags [sleeping bags], hung off the top of the stairs by their legs, and anything else you can imagine.

That should have been happening to me. Instead, I was down Limassol on the piss with the lads 'cos I was one of the boys now. I got back to battalion in the early hours of the morning. We were supposed to be gated (confined to barracks) for two weeks at this time. Cookie was on the gate, and Nobby was Provo. They'd clearly been tipped off and knew the score. They said nothing but sent me on my way back to my room. As I walked up the stairs, I saw someone hanging by their legs in their doss bag. "Thank God I didn't grass", I thought. If that's what they're doing to average recruits, what would they have done to a grass? I was pretty scared by the time I got back into my bed.

They really looked after me. I was put into a room with the most senior lads in the platoon. They'd all been serving a long time - and bear in mind, these lads had only just got back from Iraq. I knew no-one though. So when one lad walked in during the night, and I heard the door open, whilst I was still half-cut, I panicked. He told me in a Geordie or a Mackem accent (I've never really been able to tell them apart) that I'd 'be alright in here tonight'. He's a good lad, is Pete Tong.

It wasn't long before my depression started. I'd never been out of the country, away from family, for so long and there wasn't much prospect of getting back home any time soon. I just felt after the first 2-week induction cadre that I didn't like it. I was far away from home, with no personal space whatsoever, with people I didn't really know.

The first time it really hit me was when we had to go up to Agia Nikitas (or, as we called it, Aya Nic) to guard something or other in case the Turkish side of the island came up. I was on guard duty with Cushy (Jamie Cushworth). As I sat with him, we got talking. He didn't like it either. I didn't know that my feelings were depression at that time, I just felt down. It was the first time that I'd ever really thought of anything bad. We were confined into a few square metres of guard-tower, which just seemed to represent the claustrophobia of the whole thing. They'd taken our passports off us; we couldn't go home without permission. Even if we wanted to go AWOL (which we didn't), we couldn't. It's that sense of having your whole life planned out for you: having to get up when you're told, having no privacy when you shower, someone in the cubicle next to you even when you're using the toilet. There's nowhere to go, stuck in the compound for days or even weeks on end.

I saw some glass at the bottom of the barbed wire, thinking to myself that 'I could just slit my wrists right now'. I didn't mean to kill myself, just that anything would be preferable to the feeling of confinement. Anything to just get me out of there. Cushy said that he felt exactly the same. That loss of control, the feeling that there was nowhere to go; nowhere to hide. It's strange though that even now, many years after leaving the Army, I still get this sense of always having to be around someone 24/7 because back then you were always around someone. They'd be talking to you constantly even in the shower, or in the toilets. Except, I suppose, if it was Steady (Craig Stead) in the stall next door. He preferred it to be quiet, so that he could enjoy a little private alone time - just him, and his magazine (and no, I don't mean the firearm clip, obviously). He used to take ages.

All I'd ever known in life was fighting. Strangely, since joining the Army, I'd not done any actual fighting. I'd not fought, not even sparred or anything. The closest I'd come was the fracas with Oumchief months before. I hadn't joined the Army to stop fighting, but it seemed there was something missing.

"I'm getting out. I don't wanna be here", I told Steady when he was safely away from the toilets.

"Don't be daft, why?" he asked.

I told him that "I'm not enjoying it" and "I wanna box."

So he sent me to Reggie McKenzie, one of the toughest and hardest men in the battalion. Reggie was there with a Geordie bloke called Kev High. Some nicknames just write themselves. He was known as Why Aye Kev High. I told them what I'd told Steady, told them all about my amateur experience, and they said "Right, we'll sort you out".

They took me up to see Stephen Morte, who was the Regimental Serjeant-Major at the time. I was standing maybe just 5'3 or 5'4 by then, a skinny lad who hadn't even finished growing. I was left waiting outside his office, as we said in the Army, 'shitting a brick' at the thought of an interview with someone so senior.

He took one look at me and sized me up. He'd done his fair share of boxing in his time, for the Regiment, and spoke with a familiar accent coming from Conisborough. "Alright, lad, if you're any good, I'll find out."

From: Steven Morte
         Former Regimental Serjeant-Major
         Second Battalion Light Infantry

Subject: First meeting with Private Burkinshaw

At 0800 hrs on January 2, 2004, I had just finished dealing with two soldiers involved in an altercation in Limassol, Cyprus, a common occurrence.

A confident knock came at my door from my Provo [NCO Cooky] and a JNCO [Rufus]. I had tremendous respect for them and their judgement. They did not suffer fools lightly.

"Sir, we've got a young soldier outside. He asked if he could leave the Army immediately because he was promised an opportunity to box in our Battalion, Sir."

At the time due to resource commitments we were not competing as a boxing unit. Knowing my Provo and JNCO, I trusted they would not have seized the opportunity unless they believed he was worth the effort.

My responsibility was to weigh manpower issues with supporting a soldier under my command and his personal passion.

I called Private Burkinshaw in to my office. He stood barely 5'3", but spoke confidently and clearly. As an RSM I had experienced many young lads in the unit who missed home and wanted to leave. This was not the case with Private Burkinshaw. His passion for boxing was obvious.

"Sir, from being a young boy I have always had a passion for boxing, in fact I'm good at it, I've boxed in the ABAs and trained at Prince Naseem's gym. I *joined the Army, with the intent to box at a high level. I chose to come to this battalion because I was told we were the boxing battalion and that I would have the opportunity to seek to represent the Army. I have no intention of making a long career in the Army but I want to represent my unit, the Army and above all I want to make the lads and lasses proud of what I do. Since arriving I've been told this is unlikely in Cyprus as there are no boxing competitions this Year. Sir, I'm a boxer and want to pursue my career in boxing. If this isn't possible I would like to leave the Army given my young age to pursue my goal."*

I admired his honesty immediately and his confidence in stating this to a Regimental Serjeant Major known for a no-nonsense approach and for having been involved in some serious scrapes in the past.

I ordered him to report to the boxing gym in the old squash court in his gym clothes.

"Sir, I am happy to demonstrate my skills in combat if that's okay"

Corporal Rufus gave him a full workout with the pads. He proved to be a class above what I had witnessed and ever competed against in my years in the Army. I determined that we had to send him to the Army team. Being unable to provide instant guarantees, I sent him back to his Company for me to consider the options. In my mind, there was only one - the British Amy Boxing Team.

I proceeded to speak first with his Company commander, Major Winston Davis. I understood the drain on manpower, but he correctly recognised that we should give him a chance as this was a rare talent in the boxing world. The Commanding Officer, Colonel Peter Davies was also supportive. The support from the unit was second to none, top to bottom.

The Army Boxing Team was rightly very cautious. They normally only select boxers they have witnessed winning a boxing match, which in turn resulted in a call up to represent the Army. Asking them to consider Private Burkinshaw represented a risk. Chris Bessey replied:

"Sir, if you think this lad is good enough then send him to me in Aldershot for a trial. If he's an average boxer, we will send him back."

He never came back.

I secured flights, accommodation, and the trial in Aldershot, before putting him on a plane to RAF Brize Norton.

I concluded the interview by telling him "If I see you back here I will personally knock you out". He laughed at this and responded, confidently, "I won't be back but watch this space in the future". He was true to his word.

Over the years I followed Ross the Boss. We have met several times and we stayed in touch. I became Boxing officer in Germany and invited him over to present trophies as the principal guest for the inter-company boxing competition. Ross the Boss looked ever the star and was confident in the presence of any rank. He was respected by all ranks, and we are all proud to claim him as one of our own. I respect the lad completely, and am proud to report that he has become a friend.

From there, he sent me out on a trial to do some work with Corporal Jamie Rufus (Roof). Morte was taking a bit of a chance on me; he was going to be sending me down to meet the Army Boxing team back in England based on little more than word of mouth. Roof and the lads had set up a boxing gym in the squash courts a month or so earlier. Morte basically just wanted Roof to give me the once-over and prove that I wasn't going to cause him too much embarrassment by sending me back to England.

Roof had also been a good boxer in the battalion. He had me do some rounds on the bags, and then a little bit of sparring. It wasn't the longest or toughest training session I'd ever done; I'd sparred with far worse in Glyn's gym. After the session he went back to Morte, and said 'you'd better get him on a flight to England'. That was, if I remember, January 1st 2004. I was put straight on a flight on January 4th back to RAF Brize Norton to go for a trial with the Army Boxing Team.

I met yet another new group of lads. Chris Bessey MBE was the new coach, and Neil Robinson the team captain (who we called Robbo at the time, though his surname later changed to Fairclough, so he became Fiery). On the first day, Neil took me into his room with Duncan Barabou - who was a really good boxer at flyweight. I later found out that he was getting ready to leave the Army at the time.

Before this, my nickname was The Predator because I used to seek out and destroy my prey in the ring. When I showed Fiery all my pictures from the Boxing Hall of Fame, he instantly renamed me Ross The Boss. The name stuck, and I've been using it ever since.

After all this, you'd be forgiven for assuming that I made it straight into the Army Boxing Team without a problem. If you've not yet realised about the ups and downs of my life and career, nothing - and I mean nothing (except perhaps the fight for my European belt) was ever as simple as it should have been. The day after I arrived, they gave me a trial. Doing some sprints out on the track, I pulled my hamstring on the first day. It was a real blow, but thankfully they were happy to rearrange and give me another trial once the hamstring was repaired. Fiery hadn't called me Ross the Boss for nothing.

I bossed the second trial; the rest, as they say, is history.

Chapter 6

IN THE ARMY NOW

"Die with memories, not dreams"

My new base was Clayton Barracks on Thornton Road, Aldershot. It had all happened very suddenly. One day I was living in Cyprus; the next I was flying back to the UK; the next, I was living in Aldershot. Life in the Army was like that; you'd go to where you'd been ordered to go. Our accommodation was a bit rough and ready; we were placed in what was known as 'transit' accommodation. It wasn't really meant to be permanent but because we were the Army boxing team, we were stationed there permanently. It was a really old barracks, so old that on the first night there our toilets and showers didn't work. Not knowing where I was, I had to walk outside, up to another block. I was in there, brushing my teeth, and the door closed behind me.

I had a strange experience, which I still don't fully understand - I saw something like a shadow passing through me in the mirror. The entrance was directly behind me, and I could see it in the mirror. I couldn't see anyone there to cause it, so I went and opened the shower curtains. There was no-one in each of them. I kicked open the toilet doors and there was nobody there either. I thought I must have been imagining it, so I carried on brushing my teeth. Then, I thought to myself, "I didn't imagine that". I packed my bag and sprinted back out of there like there was no tomorrow. I rushed back up into my room and into my bed. There were nine of us in an eight-man room, because they'd had to create a bed space for me at short notice when I was flown back from Cyprus. I didn't know any of the lads who were there at the time, so I didn't dare tell them what had happened. They'd have thought I was a reyt fucking weirdo if I told them about something like that on the first night I met them. I still don't know what it was, but I like to think that it was a guardian angel looking over me. Being there, in Aldershot, was like a dream come true. The lads back at the battalion used to say that I was living the dream, coming back to England to box.

In many ways, that was true. I was indeed living the dream. The lads, back in the battalion, thought we had it easy. We didn't. We were training three times a day (except for the occasional half-day on Wednesdays, and being let out early for the weekend). It was brutal, going from no boxing training to training three times a day. Each session was structured like nothing I'd ever known back on civvy street. When you were at an amateur gym, you'd just turn up on the day and find out what you were doing - often depending on what mood your trainer happened to be in. In the Army, it was different. Everything was planned: our training sessions for the full week, month, and year were planned ahead to make sure we were ready for our fights. That routine, discipline, and more than anything, the structure was perfect for me.

The training sessions weren't easy. In the morning we'd go for a plod (which was a jog of up to 8 miles) or do springs, shuttle runs, or hill sprints. In the afternoon, it'd be bags, circuit classes and sparring. Our trainer, Chris Bessey, knew exactly what he was doing. He'd been a quality boxer himself; not many people become a 6-time ABA champion. He'd also won the Commonwealth gold medal and a European bronze as an amateur.

When I got to the boxing team, all I knew was how to fight. Glyn used to tell me things - move from side to side, keep your head moving, throw your jab. Glyn told you what to do; the Army made you do it. That was the difference; I needed someone to make me do things properly. Chris Bessey taught me how to box clever; how to jab and move. He made sure that I would do everything off my jab. He used to drill it into us: always go back to the mirror. Start with your jab from the chin, defending the chin. Then extend it all the way out, fully out and then snapping straight back to your chin. A proper, disciplined punch, keeping the maximum possible protection against your opponent's punches. Chris knew what he was talking about alright; his jab was perfect.

In Glyn's gym there was no-one close to my weight so I used to spar with heavier weights. Doing that used to help me in all kinds of ways, but there's a downside. If every time, you're sparring with someone much bigger than you, someone with a longer reach, you're constantly trying to move in and out. You're not always properly working behind your jab, learning to establish that jab and use it to control a fight. In the Army it would be different. There'd be someone there in each weight category. Sometimes we wouldn't just have the 'number one', but we'd also have someone there as a reserve ready to be called upon when needed. When I first started, I was boxing as a flyweight but there wasn't another flyweight there. I still had to spar with heavier guys, but sparring with a super-flyweight (Keith Spong) or bantamweight (Chris Sagar) was much closer to my weight than I'd got used to. The differences in weight are very small at those classes anyway. I'd never had that before; at around my own weight, I was finally sparring with people who'd got proper speed. It was no longer a walk in the park in the way it had been. Sparring with heavier boxers meant I was always quicker, always able to land shots - even if height, power and reach advantages would eventually outweigh speed in a proper fight.

A few months later, another flyweight came - Gareth Stemp, from the Royal Scots. I used to beat him up though. The tougher challenge was sparring with Spongy. His speed was great and he had a good chin. I felt more prepared for fights; I used to find that I'd get the chance to spar nearly every day. It was more technical stuff too. Chris or Gordon (his 'second in command') or a guy we called Rocky, would watch each round. Whilst some were on the bags or doing circuits, others would be sparring. Mistakes were picked up on instantly. We could have been twenty seconds into the round, and Chris would temporarily halt proceedings to tell us about a mistake and make sure that we knew better than to make the same mistake again. Chris would make sure that I moved side-to-side a lot more; less forward-and-back one-dimensional fighting. He'd show me and drill it into me, forcing me to put it into action. Everything he'd learned as a top-level amateur fighting with the England squad, he was determined to pass on to me.

When I'd been there for six months or so, a 17-year-old lad came and joined. He was a 57kg featherweight when he joined the team,

James Allen, from the REME (Royal Electrical and Mechanical Engineers). He was a really nice kid, and I'd never met anyone as naturally fit as him in boxing. He could run like there was no tomorrow, and in sparring he never even seemed to come up for air. It was great to have someone fresh and so good to spar with. He could move, he was fast, he could box and he could fight. He won the Combined Services championship for his own weight division and boxed in the ABAs, losing on a split decision in the semi-finals in the same year that I boxed in the final.

Years later, and unsurprisingly, he won an ABA title at bantamweight. I've often thought that he'd have made a really good career for himself if he'd turned professional. The thing about James, though, is that he was committed to the Army first and foremost, through and through. At the time of writing he's still in the Army. He's now the Army Boxing Team coach, and I couldn't imagine anyone better to be filling Chris Bessey's substantial shoes.

At Glyn's gym there was a sense of togetherness and teamwork, but that was nothing compared to what we had in the Army. We lived together; we ate together; we slept just 2 feet apart. There was just a 2-foot cabinet separating our beds, with lockers either side of us. When you're living in the same room as your team-mates, it makes you closer as a team as well. We'd always be looking out for everyone else's results. We'd have a sense of pride in ourselves as a team, a mentality of the 'army against civvies' behind everything we were doing. You'd never want to let anyone get one over on you. When we won, it reflected well on the Army. When we lost, it reflected badly on the Army. It pushed us on to do more. Everything in the Army was designed to do that, to make us 'Be The Best' as the recruiting posters used to always say.

My fitness levels were unbelievable. I could literally have taken on the world with that fitness. It was that standard of training that I held myself up to when I was training for twelve-rounders later in my career. I used the skills I'd learned in the Army to make sure that I didn't slack in my later career as a professional. I used to ask myself 'what would I be like if Bessey was watching me now?'. Or, when I was running on my own as a professional, if my civvy bezzie Carl Wild wasn't with me, I wondered what Treacle would be saying.

Treacle was my best mate from the Army Boxing Team. He was 5 or 6 years older than me, Lance-Corporal Jason Summers. We nicknamed him 'Treacle' because he was a proper Cockney. He could hear the Bow Bells (the bells of St Mary-le-Bow, Cheapside, City of London) from his house, which is the true definition of a cockney. Finally, I wasn't alone: I'd found another Del Boy - no wonder he became my best mate. He'd got himself a girlfriend, he'd been around a bit, so I suppose I looked up to him and respected him. I saw him as being like the older brother I never had just as much as being my best mate.

Don't get me wrong, the Army boxing training is pretty tough, but we'd take it one step further and do the extra round. Me and Treacle would still be a member of Fitness First. We'd go to the gym in the evening, doing another session on the cross-trainers and treadmills, then get in the sauna, chatting and putting the world to rights.

Gen was on the opposite side of my bed to Treacle. He used to go out every Tuesday or Wednesday night. He loved sex, and he had the right equipment to prove it. He'd meet people online and do the whole cuckold type thing: he'd go and sleep with wives whilst their husbands watched. Sometimes he'd take even one or two of the lads with him. I'm not gonna mention their names because some of them are married now.

We'd all be back at Clayton Barracks (or as we called it, The Lodge). Gen would come back either that evening, or the middle of the night, or even turn back up the next day just before training. We'd hear all the stories about how some guy would be sitting in front of the wardrobe while he rattled the guy's missus.

Years later, I'm told that some of the lads had just come back after a particularly tough tour of Afghanistan. They were relaxing in true Army fashion, knocking one out to a porno. Their enjoyment was interrupted by seeing Gen on screen. Gen was now a porn star. I suppose all us Army lads wanted to Be The Best, and Gen had reached the top in his own career.

One day we'd had our end-of-season party. It was down at the sports track, where we did our runs every morning. We were allowed to use the conference room down there which had a bar. After a few drinks, we were all pretty half-cut before we set out into town. We got taxis down there, before the usual thing happened - we all ended up getting into a bit of a ruck. The fight was like something you'd see in a comic strip. It was pretty much the whole Army Boxing Team against civvies; one punch and people were down, time and time again. The carnage left behind us was pretty impressive, but I'm not so sure that the police were that impressed. Treacle and Jamie gave me some pretty sound advice: don't say anything, don't tell them nothing, don't even tell them who you are.

So when the police asked me "Who are you? You're not from round here?", I responded that I was Ross Burkinshaw, from the Army Boxing Team. "Are you any good?", they asked me.

"I've just become Combined Services Champion and I'm an ABA finalist. Google me!" I couldn't have ignored Jamie and Treacle's advice any worse if I'd tried. They put their heads in their hands. Fortunately they only kept us overnight, and no-one got charged. Once we'd all sobered up, they let us out the day after. By that time Treacle wasn't there, but Jamie was.

"Why the fuck did you tell them that last night?", he asked. I couldn't remember a thing, but I replied "At least I'm more famous now". Even back then, I always loved people knowing my name. That kind of fight was a regular occurrence, especially when it was me, Jamie and Treacle heading into town for a session on the booze.

My Army boxing career started with a junior fight in the junior ABAs. I beat a kid from Bournemouth and became Southern Area champion. It was, I suppose, the first reward for the Army believing in me: one fight, one title. Then, I boxed a lad from the tough Spennymoor gym. I think his name was James McIlveney. Everyone said that I'd got robbed on points. It didn't take long in that environment before I started winning titles at amateur level. My ambition to turn professional never let me get beyond Combined Services champion and Southern Area champion as an amateur though. Those days really were some of the best of my life. I was doing the thing I loved most in the world (I'd not met Kelly by then), with some of the best people I've ever had the privilege to meet. It wasn't quite all work and no play like it had been in the Regiment either. Sometimes they'd give us an early finish on a Friday, or even on a Thursday afternoon on occasion, so that we could go back and see family and friends. So long as we made 'sure you were ready for a hard session first thing Monday morning', we were okay.

For me, that meant training over the weekends too. I'd always go back and spend time training in Glyn's gym. I loved training with the Army, and I loved training with Glyn. The two were poles apart in approach, but I learned so much from both of them. I still remember some of the incredible times I'd had at Glyn's gym. Those were the days!

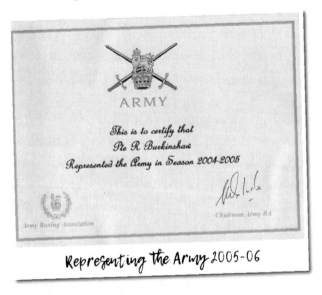

ARMY

This is to certify that
Pte R Burkinshaw
Represented the Army in Season 2004-2005

Chairman Army BA

Army Boxing Association

Representing the Army 2005-06

Chapter 7

GLYN'S GYM

If there's one thing I can say about Glyn's gym, it's that we always looked out for one another. We'd give anything to make sure that everyone else was looked after, always putting each other first. I'll tell you though, the stuff we used to get up to was a bit shocking. It was in the days before anyone had invented stuff like child protection, and I was a really cheeky kid. Friends are still commenting on how cheeky I was even today. Glyn's approach to this kind of thing was a bit rough and ready. It grew me up. If I was cheeky to someone, I'd get a clip round the ear. It was a different generation, he'd never do anything like that now and I'd never do 'owt like that in my gym either.

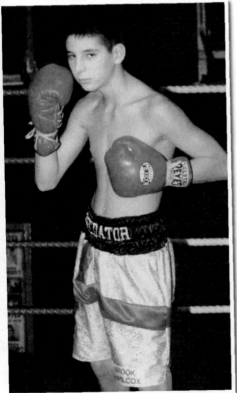

Ross boxing amateur

He'd just give as good as he got, which is actually a great lesson for boxing in a funny sort of way. Our pranks were a bit over the top. One of our favourite 'games' was heating spoons in cups of coffee then burning each other on the back of the neck with the hot spoons. Glyn had an amazing separate amateur setup at the time I joined. He'd worked with Harry Cliffe (who was our matchmaker), Bob Cotterill (the gym's amateur coach), and was later joined by Frank Middleton (a great coach who'd been round different top gyms). Frank was like a grandfather figure to me, someone that all of us truly respected. He knew me to be a Del Boy type, and he always used to affectionately say that by the time I was 30, I'd either be locked up or a millionaire. For some reason, I always wanted to choose the millionaire route. Frank was just someone everyone could relate to and get along with. He'd been with lots of gyms round Sheffield over the years, spent lots of time with Brendan Ingle, and had some amazing stories to tell. I used to love listening to him, absorbing the little details of boxing life.

A British Army regiment (23 Pioneer) used to travel up from Bicester, to train in our gym. Their coach was Pat Sheehan, a friend of Herol 'Bomber' Graham. He saw a few of the junior boxers training, and was really impressed with us. Pat used to put on shows down at the Army camp in Oxfordshire, and decided to ask Frank if he could put a few of us juniors on his next boxing bill. Me, Dwayne and Richard Hill were chosen to make the journey down. We travelled down with their parents, my parents, and of course Harry and Frank. It really opened my eyes to a different world: this was easily the best amateur boxing show I'd ever boxed on. I was maybe about 14 years old at the time. We were treated like royalty, our parents were properly wined and dined in the Officers' Mess, and we got to box. Nothing could have been better. They found another civvy junior from Lincoln for me to fight, and I won of course. I enjoyed winning. Looking back now, I wonder whether that experience was the first time the thought of joining the Army had been planted in my head. After all, there aren't that many careers where you get paid to do what you love. Years later, one of the senior boxers from that Regiment came and trained with the Army boxing team. He recognised me from fighting on their show when I was a junior, and from coming up to train with us at Glyn's gym, and he's still on my Facebook now. It's a small world. When I won the English title much later, I took the belt round to Frank's house to show him. He was so proud of me.

My mate Carl Wild was just easily led, he'd do 'owt I'd say. Carl was always tall, but had this daft mushroom haircut. It was little and large. I was 4 foot but he was 6 foot, and his mum always used to ask me to watch him. She'd ask me 'Will you watch him crossing the road?' and stuff like that. She'd only ever give him £5 notes, which didn't make much sense to me. I asked her 'Why do you only give Carl fivers?'. She said that she didn't trust him with more than £5 because he doesn't bother to check his change. He's a great mate, but I did lead him into a few scrapes.

One day we were with a kid who we called 'back-foot Eddie' because he'd always fight on the defensive. We were inventive with nicknames like that. So we'd got Carl to burn him with the spoon, he'd done it to Carl and Wainy back, as you do. I wasn't having anyone pick on my mates (and yeah, I know, we'd started it) so I put the spoon on hot sauna coals, and used a towel to lift it off so I could burn his leg with it. He got the biggest blister you'd ever seen. We were a handful for Glyn to try to control, to say the least. Once when I was about 13 or 14, at the end of the boxing season, we'd gone down to an Italian restaurant just down the road from the gym to celebrate. I'd been doing the spoon thing all evening, annoying them because I just wouldn't quit. One of the pro fighters said he'd get me back, and I didn't listen to him. I did it again. He certainly kept his word. He heated a knife on the candle on the table, before putting the knife across the back of my neck. It was so hot that it didn't even feel hot. "Ah, you didn't even get me!" I taunted him. Then, the pain kicked in. All the skin started peeling off in my hand. I've still got the scar to prove it from that evening. That's just what happened in them days. It wa' just a laugh.

Another time, this guy called Macca came in to train. On the weekends, I used to train then work on the counter for Glyn taking money. One day, it was a bit quiet so when Macca came in we let the tyres down on his bike. A bit later, as we were leaving, Carl started screaming 'Ross, he's got me!'. Macca just held Carl hostage till I went to Morrisons to get his tyres pumped back up. Carl didn't think I was coming back, but whether it's the Army or boxing or just life in general, you don't leave your mates behind. Carl was a cracking mate, we used to sleep over at each other's houses all the time. When it came to my wedding, I even had him as my best man. No hot spoons on that day though.

Most of my stories from that time involve Carl in one way or another. One time we went go-karting near Sheffield Ski Village. After we were done, the trainers went on and had a go. We got bored, so we started chucking stones at their helmets. We thought it was funny for longer than they did, so they started chasing us all the way down the hill from the ski village. They caught Carl and chucked him in the river Don to get him back. I managed to get back to the gym, thinking I'd got to safety, but they'd not forgotten. They kept chasing me so I sprinted across the car park, and went up the drainpipe onto the roof. Nobody could climb up after, so they stood waiting for me to get back down. It was an hour and a half of stalemate as they stood at the bottom, waiting to get me back. It was only ended when Glyn's missus Hilary at that time pulled up in her car. She made them leave me alone so I could climb down.

It was all in good fun, but it taught me some discipline in an odd sort of way. I learned from Glyn's gym how you couldn't get away with stuff. Nobody really stood up to me before in that way, and today in the 21st century people would scream all kinds of stuff about people taping me up and tying me to the ropes of the boxing ring and stuff. Two things made a bigger difference to making me into a man than anything else: Glyn's gym, and the Army. We'd mess about a lot, but when it came down to it, we'd always look out for each other. I'd be doing anything I could to make a bit of extra cash on the side, so I used to help sell tickets for Glyn's professional boxing shows. Glyn always used to say 'there's only one thing worse than being skint, and that's looking skint'. One day, someone had come in with a few knocked-off mobile phones. As a kid, we used to call them 'bat phones' - they'd have unlimited credit on. So this one day, I had a few mobiles on me and thousands of pounds worth of tickets when the gym closed at 12. Me and Wainy got on the tram to Meadowhall. Henry Cooper was doing a book signing there, so we were desperate to go and meet him. A load of lads got on the tram, and it was absolutely heaving. It looked like a full football team, and they kept staring at us. I'm not stupid, I could sense a bit of tension right away. They started shouting abuse at us. I told Wainy to ignore 'em, to put the rucksack on and fasten it tight to him. I told him I'd sort it, and they'd have to get through me if they wanted to get to him.

A few of them waited behind on the tram. It was clear they were trying some kind of ambush, but there were people around so we walked straight past them and upstairs. As we got onto the bridge going over to Meadowhall, they were shouting loads of abuse and getting closer to us. I told Wainy 'reyt, get ready'. I had a long-sleeved top on, so I rolled my sleeves up. "Look at him thinking he's hard", they said. I didn't think I was hard. I knew I was hard. "Who are you talking to? You're the ones that's been shouting abuse at us", I said. As they came forward to attack us, I hit the first one and the two mates next to him. We proper battered them, but security came very quickly. They'd seen us on the camera and they'd been following us. Because we'd been acting in self-defence, they were the ones that got kicked out and we carried on with our afternoon at Meadowhall. The stakes were high; I didn't want to miss out on meeting Henry Cooper!

I'd been determined that nobody was going to get that bag off us because of the tickets and mobiles. I couldn't imagine having to tell Glyn that we'd got ourselves robbed of thousands of pounds of his tickets. I'd never have lived it down. Still, I'm glad that security didn't search us…

We used to go down to Devon and box down there. They'd

arrange matches: Sheffield Boxing Centre v Bideford Select. We'd all get put up in different houses to stay over. You've no idea how much trouble we used to get up to in the minibus. It was like a school trip on steroids. We'd be messing about, mooning and rodding passing cars. Then there was what we used to call 'garrotting' - when we'd half-strangle whichever adult was in the passenger seat from behind, using their seatbelt. Anyone daring to fall asleep on the long journey would wake up differently to how they fell asleep. They'd have toothpaste everywhere or I'd use a pen to write all over Fewky's head. Fewky's dad, Big John, was often the driver. Harry, our matchmaker, was really old-school. We used to think that he was a grumpy old man but he wasn't really - it's just how he came across to us kids, largely because we spent so much time winding him up. I'd be grumpy if I was him, knowing how much we used to wind him up. One time whilst we were down there, we were sitting down in the living room watching something on TV. Carl Wild had a TV-remote watch, one of the gadgets at the time. I got hold of it, hid in the doorway, and used it to change the TV channel every time Harry started to watch something. He'd be banging the remote, tapping the telly, and then I'd do it again just as he settled back down. After a while he heard me laughing, looked round and saw me and Carl hiding in the doorway. That's one of those moments I won't forget in a hurry, him as a 70-odd year-old man running at me and doing a flying kick at me. From that day, his new nickname was Harry Van Damme.

My best fight during my time in Devon was a one-round stoppage. I decided to come out to Hot Chocolate - You Sexy Thing, because Herol 'Bomber' Graham had come out to the same track when he fought Vinnie Pazienza at London's Wembley stadium. Because I knocked my opponent out in the first round, I always said that I'd use that song as my ring entrance music when I was a pro. For some reason I never did. But then, when I came home to Sheffield to fight at the Octagon Centre for the European belt, the time was right. I put that music back on, knocked my opponent out in the first round, and picked up the European title.

It was a different age. I wish I could tell you a few more stories from back in those days, but I don't want to get anyone into trouble for doing anything to me that I totally deserved at the time. I've got to be careful because of political correctness and all that stuff. I don't want people being judged today on what they did in a different era, 20 years ago. The story about the stun gun or what I did to Joe Woodhouse with a spoon (and I tell you now, it wasn't burning his *neck*)? Sorry, we're just going to have to leave those stories to your imagination for now. As a professional, Glyn used to look after me too. He was as much a mate as a trainer, so one time he took me on holiday to Tenerife. We went to scout out a venue for a potential training camp, TKO Boxing. That's where I met my conditioning coach, Michael Lovett, before my English title. He was really up on everything to do with getting into shape for peak performance: nutrition, diet, strength and conditioning. At times in the run-up to a fight we used to speak daily, because I was always checking what I could and couldn't eat. What I've learned from him, I find myself passing on now to my clients who come in to my gym. I can't thank him enough for what he did for me. As for Glyn, well, the whole 'hot spoon' trick never gets old. Even last year, he was still up to it with some of his mates in a local restaurant.

Chapter 8

THE EDGE OF GLORY

In my first year down at Aldershot with the Army Boxing Team, I boxed as a junior. There wasn't a Combined Services competition for juniors, so I didn't get that experience until I was old enough to do it in the second season. It's an experience you don't easily forget; the Army, Navy and RAF coming together to box each other. The venue would rotate from one year to the next, and this year it was the turn of the Navy to host it so we headed down to the naval base at HMS Nelson. Victory was all that mattered. The Army hadn't lost a Combined Services for many years; we always had more Army champions than Navy or RAF, usually more Army than Navy and RAF put together. It was a source of pride for us to be the champions; we couldn't let the

Ross with the Army Boxing Team

team down. The record continued until last year (2018) when the Army finally lost after 34 consecutive victories.

The Combined Services
Individual & Team
BOXING CHAMPIONSHIPS
2005

to be held at
THE GYMNASIUM
HMS NELSON
THURSDAY 10th FEBRUARY 2005

1830 - Doors open
1930 - Boxing commences

Refreshments Available - Retain this ticket at all times

0900

ALL SEATS £5.00

Becoming Combined Services champ

In each weight division, the winner would become the Combined Services champion and represent all three Forces in the ABA finals. There was nobody at super-flyweight fighting for the RAF, so it was a straightforward fight between me and Max Khan, the Navy's champion. Some of my family went down to watch me.

Any military boxing show is more spectacular than civilian amateur shows. I try sometimes to explain it to civvies, and they just don't get it at all. It's something you have to experience in order to understand it. Everything is run in a precise, military, regimented manner. The timings are like clockwork, varied only when there's a stoppage or something happens in the ring to cause a slight variation. The entrance music is grand, military, old-fashioned and with the 19th-century vibe you

From Lieutenant Colonel H E Shields MBE

2nd Battalion The Light Infantry
NIBAT!
British Forces Post Office 811

CO/DO

Private Burkinshaw

8 January 2005

Dear Private Burkinshaw,

AWARD OF BATTALION SPORTS COLOURS

I am delighted to inform you that you have been awarded Battalion Sports Colours for your significant achievements in Boxing. On behalf of All Ranks, I offer you my warmest congratulations. The awards were announced on Christmas Day here in Northern Ireland to much acclaim.

The Sports Colours are in the form of a framed certificate giving your name and the sport for which you were awarded your Colours. Your Sports Colours are currently sitting in the RSM's office here in Bessbrook Mill. Would you please call the RSM[1] in order to let him know whether you want your Colours to be sent to you in the post or when you will be in Edinburgh (post 17 March 2005) in order for me to formally present your Colours to you. The latter option is preferred but I appreciate that our programmes might not coincide!

Once again, well done and my warmest congratulations to you.

well done! We hope to send someone to see your next fight. Keep up the good work!

Ted Shields.

might associate with something like Sharpe or Hornblower. Everything is professional, in the way you'd expect the Armed Forces to deliver. Compared with most amateur boxing, it's on a much grander scale - the atmosphere is more like professional than amateur, but with a very different kind of atmosphere in the crowd. Everything happens in a ceremonial manner; boxers entering the ring to the sound of the drums, bugles, or bagpipes.

When the officer in the centre of the ring speaks, everything goes silent. This isn't like the MC of a professional fight, drowning everyone out with the sound of the microphone. It's the calm before the storm; a silence that envelops the venue, the quiet decorum and British stiff upper lip before we whack seven bells out of each other.

Like a minute's silence at a football stadium, the hush is observed as the officer announces the action. Then, it's over. The bell rings, and it's the start of Round 1. Just like the football match, when the referee's whistle signals the end of a silence and the start of the action, the crowd cheers. The atmosphere is so much more electric for the contrast between silence and action.

Yet unlike a football match, neither booing nor jeering is permitted. Both boxers are servicemen representing branches of Her Majesty's Armed Forces; respect is deserved and demanded. We cheer on those we support; we do not jeer those whose job it is to keep and enforce the Queen's peace.

I came out of my corner, straight into action, a young lad barely old enough to compete as an adult, facing the finest the Navy could muster. I annihilated him; the referee had already given him two warnings for holding and two counts before he stopped the contest after just 1 minute and 40 seconds of the first round; I was now the Combined Services champion.

That conversion from boy to man, the natural step up and the fight in such a venue, made me think 'Yes, I've made it now'. I had indeed made it; I'd made it straight through to the semi-finals of the ABA [Amateur Boxing Association] National Championships of 2005. The Combined Services bout was, effectively, the quarter-finals of the ABA Championships. At this point, as luck would have it, my semi-final opponent was unable to compete so I got a walkover into the final.

The final of the ABA National Championships was a pretty big deal, televised live on the BBC. My mate Brett Fourney from the Army Boxing Team had also made it to the final in his weight class. If I was going to box in the finals of the ABAs, I'd picked the right year for it: some of today's household names were on that bill - Tony Bellew, Jamie Cox, James DeGale and David Price. Tony Jeffries would, I think, have joined them had hand injuries not forced him to retire undefeated after just ten professional fights. Michael Robinson, who I would later box as a professional, was also there.

The only thing this event had in common with the Combined Services was that it was much grander than the usual amateur bills. It was held at the Excel Arena in London with an atmosphere that was electric. A coachload of my fans travelled down to watch me. There were a few thousand people in that venue, more than you'd see at quite a lot of fights. In fact, there were more people watching me in the finals of the amateur competition than were there, years later, when I fought Jason Cunningham to win the Commonwealth title. It's a strange world.

My opponent in the final was Stuart Langley. His identical twin, Darren, was boxing in the weight class below, so there was lots of emphasis on them in the media building up to March 5th, 2005, the date of the 118th ABA finals. If two identical twins won, it'd be a massive story; something like that doesn't happen every day! I felt like the pressure was on. It was the biggest pressure I'd felt in boxing so far, not least because of the press interest in my opponent's story. I had a massive dressing room for that fight, with Chris Bessey and Fiery there for me. I was the second fight on, at super-flyweight. Darren, who boxed out of the Hollington gym like his brother, was fighting first. He boxed and won comfortably. I knew I'd have my work cut out that night.

At the time, I was only 18 years old, barely old enough to be there. The other ABA lads respected us Army lads; they knew that we were supremely fit, and that we could box. Stuart was much older and far more experienced than I was, already on the England team. I went out there and put everything into it, but I really wasn't suited for the amateur style of point-scoring. It was a computer scoring system; I'd rather take a shot to land a harder one, but that was useless for accumulating points. I felt like I'd done okay, but my punches just didn't count on the system in the way my opponent's did so he got the win by a pretty wide margin. I've got no regrets at all about that fight. All I could do was my best, and I can hand on heart say there's nothing more I could have done.

Ross with Audley Harrison

Some of the lads from the Army would end up on the Great Britain squad at the time, which meant there was a connection between us and some of the big names. Audley Harrison was the big name in British boxing at the time. He'd won the Olympic gold medal before turning professional and winning the WBF heavyweight title. His fights were televised on the BBC, and with terrestrial TV comes name recognition. It was a big moment for us when Audley came down to our gym to train with us and do a bit of a press and media show. I got on well with him, and he took me on the pads as part of the exhibition for the media. I was a super-flyweight demonstrating my skills to an Olympic super-heavyweight; the picture looks like a David and Goliath moment or perhaps something out of a cartoon.

At the end of the boxing season, all the lads would have to go back to their battalions. The only exception was if you'd won the Combined Services title for your weight division and made the Combined Services team. In that case, you'd be able to stay at Aldershot with the Combined Services team and they would try to arrange an international fight. They always used to say 'join the Navy and see the world', but I spent my fair share of time travelling with the Army. Those were great days, going on tour with the lads. In 2005, they arranged for the Army Boxing Team to go and fight against the Austrian international team. We saw it as a bit of a holiday, a reward for a job well done, but at the same time we took it seriously because we knew we were boxing as well. I was just excited to see what it was like, competing abroad and visiting a new country.

Army Boxing Team in Austria

When we got to our hotel, a couple of the lads were a little over the weight. Dean 'Frosty' Frost had been on the team for years, had been round the block a bit and knew all the tricks of the trade as well as his experience in the ring. At that time, we didn't have the sports science support to tell us precisely how to lose weight so we'd do whatever we could to get the weight to come off. We were due to go down for the weigh-in and meet our opponents. Me and Treacle, Spongy and Fiery were all outside and worrying about making the weight.

Warning: Do Not Try This At Home! Frosty told us "I've got a new trick. It's reyt good for getting weight off. We've just got to do you a personalised colonic irrigation."

It turned out that he'd tried this before. You'd squirt a water bottle up your arse, hold it in for as long as you could, and then go to the toilet. He reckoned it'd flush out all the waste that was in there and you'd lose the weight.

"Look, there's a hosepipe there. Hold it towards your ring piece, bend over, and I'll turn the tap on steady." I was pretty desperate, so I did as he said. I could feel it going around and up through my internals. He said hold it as much as you can, then run to the toilet. I held it for as long as I could, then realised I had to go. I sprinted to the toilet, little 'rabbit droppings' following behind me. I was now desperate in the other sense of the word. I kicked the door open, and Chris Bessey was sitting on the toilet. I pushed him off, leaving him sitting on the floor in a heap, and let everything rip.

As the contents of my intestines started spewing out, so did the swear words from the mouth of Chris Bessey. "What the fuck are you doing, Ross?" It took me a while to be able to explain, but he still wasn't massively impressed. Thankfully, when it had all calmed down, he saw the funny side afterwards.

Maybe Frosty was right after all. I made the weight. After all that, though, my opponent pulled out. I'd gone through it all for absolutely nothing. It now became just a holiday for me; I could have a good drink and support the other lads in training. I spent time taking them on the pads.

We got the chance to go up the mountains. I was scared of heights back then. I'm over that now - my recent sky-dive cured me of that. We had to go up in some rickety old chair lifts, with just a bar to hold you in. Treacle kept bouncing up and down, whilst we were what seemed hundreds of feet high in the air. I was going mental. It was absolutely brilliant.

The following year, our end-of-term trip was to Canada and plenty more jollies. Boxing was what we were good at, but we were even better at partying. We were due to fight against the Canadian national boxing team. We arrived in Edmonton, the home of the world's biggest shopping mall, and stayed at an Army camp up in the hills in a place called Medicine Hat.

Amazingly, the same thing happened again for the second year in a row. I could see and hear lots of whispering going on. Bessey, Fiery, Robbo and a few of their coaches were talking together. I kept seeing them look at me. I could tell that something was up, and they came over to talk to me. "Everyone's on...except you and Dilksy", they told me. Lightning had struck twice; my opponent had pulled out. It was yet another walkover. I was very lucky because it became another free holiday, but actually I was gutted. I was a boxer; I wanted to box. Dilksy ended up following in my footsteps. He turned pro later too, and did pretty well in the Prizefighter competition on Sky Sports.

"Listen lads, you've got a 2-week paid holiday now. Enjoy it." We didn't need any more invitation than that. We had a hired minibus, and the lads who were boxing couldn't drink too much so there was no shortage of designated drivers. Each night, we'd get driven in to Calgary to go to different bars. They absolutely loved us down there. Everyone wanted to meet us; they'd heard the Army Boxing Team was over. I really can't figure out why but for some reason, the sight of British soldiers from the Army Boxing Team was quite popular with the girls out in Calgary. One bar was a bit like Coyote Ugly - barmaids dancing on the tables, and giant ice bins of Bud or Corona. We were dancing on a little stage, and this guy kept bumping into me. I wouldn't normally shy away from a confrontation but Dilksy stepped in. Before I knew it, Dilksy had his head on the guy's nose and warning him "Don't mess with the boss!". Across the room, I heard one local shout "Whoa, man! He's using his head". That's not what they were expecting of boxers. They absolutely loved us in there. So even Dilksy got a fight on that trip but I didn't.

I've always loved some of the Kenny Rogers songs, like The Gambler.

"You gotta know when to hold 'em, know when to fold 'em, know when to walk away, know when to run. You never count your

money when you're sitting at the table. There'll be time enough for counting, when the dealing's done."

You know what? Boxing's a bit like that. When you're on top in a fight, you've got to know when to press your advantage, when to look for the knockout, and when to just take the win on points. No point chalking up a win until the referee stops the contest or your hand is raised in victory after a hard-fought battle.

I was drunk one night in a taxi on the way back from a good night out, and the taxi driver started telling me a story about how he'd met Kenny Rogers - and gambled with The Gambler in Vegas. I don't know whether I believe him or not, but I'll never forget the story.

We really did have the time of our lives on that trip; we got an adventure training package thrown in. You name it, we did it. White water rafting, horseback riding in the Canadian Rockies, mountain climbing, canoeing. One of the lads, Stan, had always been scared of horses. We talked him round. It's a once in lifetime chance; you may never be back in the Canadian Rockies again, you're getting this for free but some people would pay thousands for it, and so on.

Having guilt-tripped him into it, finally Stan got up on his horse. He kept saying "Take it steady, whoa, whoa". I got my horse next to his, and - as horses tend to do when they're next to each other, they started running faster. I gave his horse a quick kick up the arse for good measure. It galloped faster and went straight into a tree. That one didn't go down too well, let me tell you. It almost broke bones in his hand, and this was before his fight!

They were great times. I suppose it's fitting to quote Bryan Adams, the Canadian singer-songwriter in the song Summer of 69:

"Oh when I look back now, that summer seemed to last forever. And if I had the choice, Yeah I'd always wanna be there. Those were the best days of my life."

In late 2004, we'd been given 2 weeks' leave from the Army Boxing Team. They said we could go on holiday if we wanted, so the next day me, Chris Sagar and David Hodkinson (Hoggy) booked ourselves some flights to Turkey. We'd told them we were on the Army Boxing Team and wanted to go somewhere lively to have a good time. I'd only just turned 18 but they were older, so we were looking for a typical 18-30s holiday. They told us there's a place called Kemer in Turkey which would be right up our alley.

Of course we said yeah, taking the first thing that they'd offered. Two days later we were on our way to the airport. We left the car at Hoggy's in Rochdale, and his dad dropped us at airport. We were the last drop off on the coach. It went into mountains, twisting and winding, giving us travel sickness and everything. Finally it came down the other side of the mountain, to a small a place on its own. It was a bit like Stocksbridge: a small town in the middle of nowhere. I can get away with saying that 'cos I'm from Stocksbridge. We checked into the hotel. It was full of old people and pensioners everywhere. Let's just say that this wasn't quite the 18-30s holiday we'd had in mind.

There was literally nowt to do in the complex and no girls to chat up. We had to make the best of it, so we checked ourselves into the hotel and got up to start on the drinks. We picked up the cocktails menu. Because it was an all-inclusive deal, there wasn't much else to do but drink and we kept on downing the cocktails.

We went to have a chat with the holiday rep to ask what was going on. She told us that it was 'geriatric weekend' at the hotel. Time to get on the cocktails properly. "They're alreyt, these", Sagar said. "I feel pissed already", Hoggy replied. We were drinking those cocktails all day.

By the third day, the holiday was getting even worse. We went to an expensive restaurant, the food was terrible and we couldn't afford to pay the bill. We said we'd do a runner, and Hoggy was even faster than we were. He suggested that me and Sagar should leave, whilst he would head out of the bathroom window. We sprinted out of the door. By the time I ran out of breath, nobody was following us. We waited and waited. Eventually, Hoggy caught up with us. He couldn't fit through the bathroom window, so he had to pay the bill himself.

Back at the hotel, bored out of our brains, we kept on at the cocktails. I picked up the menu to look at some of them in more detail. Turned out that the free drinks we'd been having for days were non-alcoholic. We'd thought we were getting pissed, but it was just the placebo effect: we were getting nothing stronger than a sugar high.

Chapter 9

BOSS BOX PRO

It had to happen eventually: my Battalion pointed out to the Army Boxing Team that they hadn't seen me for a couple of years, and that it was high time I went back and did some actual work. I rolled up my sleeves, put on my green uniform, and started doing some proper soldiering for the first time in years. There were a few things going down at the time: Northern Ireland was due to come up for us, so we were busy with riot training, and the situation in Lebanon was getting worse by the day.

Because I'd been away with the Army Boxing Team, they kept picking me up on everything and putting me straight into the action. My platoon sergeant Smudge (Craig Smith) was doing riot training with us. He said "We'll have Burky as front man". Fair enough, but I weighed 8 stone. Other regiments were playing the civvies, and they were all big men. They weren't messing about either. We'd have our shields and batons, then they'd attack. They'd pick on me, because I was small and in front. They'd drag me in, and the other lads would have to get me out of there. I got myself more cuts and bruises doing that than I ever did with the boxing team.

It was all over the news about Lebanon; things were really kicking off there. They put our Regiment on spearhead, which meant that we had just a few hours' notice to move anywhere in the world. I was excited - all I'd really known of the Army was the boxing side of it. Whenever anyone from the Regiment saw me, they'd call me a 'tracksuit soldier' because I'd done very little proper soldiering. Nobby would say "He's here, the tracksuit soldier. What the fuck are you doing in uniform? Are you feeling okay?" They respected me though. Everyone, even the Regimental Serjeant Major, called me by my first name. I was no longer Private Burkinshaw as you'd expect of a soldier. I was Ross, or Burky, or Ross the Boss, one of the Regiment's biggest assets and something of a superstar in the Battalion.

Even so, I was looking forward to going: this was my chance to prove to the lads that I wasn't just a tracksuit soldier. Running my gym, I might have been grafting for 12 hours a day, but my ex-wife Nicola never quite saw it as a proper job - maybe because I genuinely love what I do. I wouldn't want to be stuck in a job I hate. In the Army Boxing Team, the training was intense, bordering on brutal. But I couldn't expect the lads with the Battalion to appreciate that; some of them were bound to think I was just having a bit of a lark at the Army's expense - though I'd like to have seen *them* try the levels of fitness we needed to have to box for the Army.

We got called to muster. It was clearly serious; you could pick up the vibe that something was going on. Once we were all out on parade, the Colonel himself addressed us: "Lads, you've seen on the news. Shit's just got real. One of the companies is going to go out and start extracting British personnel from Lebanon."

I was in A Company at the time. A Company and C Company were told to get ready and were put on 3 hours' notice. C Company were sent out there first. In the meantime, some General from the Army Boxing Team heard that we were on the point of being deployed. He phoned my Colonel and said "Ross isn't to go. We need him back in Aldershot, straight away." They didn't want me getting wounded. I was one of the golden boys for the Army. I used to win the Combined Services. I'd got letters from Brigadiers congratulating me. They needed me for next year.

I went home, on a long weekend. I was speaking to Glyn Rhodes, and he told me about my mate Fewky turning pro with Frank Maloney. I wanted to do the same thing, so Glyn had a chat with Frank. Frank had seen me on the Army Boxing Team; he'd love to have me.

There was a problem though: under Army rules, you couldn't earn 2 wages at the same time. I was no longer eligible to leave the Army; I hadn't yet done my minimum 4 years from my 18th birthday. After the long weekend, I went down and did a few more weeks of training but it was still playing on my mind. Any lads who'd turned pro before whilst serving in the Army had technically gone AWOL. That wasn't the route I'd have wanted to go down, and I doubt it'd have been good for a promoter either. The Army had a retention problem: they'd lost so many assets over recent years - people like Kelly Holmes, Nigel Benn, and various football and rugby players. They couldn't afford to keep losing them, so something was going to have to change.

I called my Regiment, and went in front of my Adjutant. He spoke to the Colonel and explained the situation. Soon, a new ruling came out - anyone wanting to follow sport in a professional manner was now allowed. That was my opportunity. I was the first to do it, though others quickly followed suit.

"Where do you want to train?"

"In Sheffield, in Glyn Rhodes' gym"

They made me sign a contract which made it clear that my Army career was paramount to my boxing career. I became the first serving soldier ever to be granted permission to become a professional boxer. Lads like Pacy and Brett had left the Army to go pro, but Amir would later follow in my footsteps by combining the two. I was ordered to go back to Sheffield and told that my Regiment would be in touch.

After my English title win

All my dreams were coming true. It wa' fucking mega. I got back, started training, got my first fight lined up. As a boxer at any level, everything's left to the managers, promoters and trainers pretty much. A boxer might have an opinion, but more often than not they'd just ignore you. As a young boxer starting out in the professional ranks, I trusted my team to arrange the right fights. From the promoter's point of view, it's straightforward and simple. Money talks. If the money's there and it's right for your career, the fight happens. If not, it doesn't.

The match was made. The die was cast. Robert Bunford would be my first professional opponent.

Chapter 10

FIGHTING OUTSIDE THE SQUARE RING

I was young, dumb and broke - just like the song. Once I'd started boxing professionally, I shouldn't have been broke but that's a different story. If you're a young would-be professional boxer reading this, I've got one warning for you. Don't get involved in fighting out on the streets. If I hadn't, you wouldn't be reading this book right now. I wouldn't be ready to write my autobiography yet because I'd be world champion and far too busy defending my title.

They say that injuries come from boxing, but mine were more often caused by fighting in the streets. I guess that's always the way of it though. When it's regulated, with proper gloves, weight restrictions, a referee and paramedics at ringside, boxers are properly protected. Streetfighting without gloves, knuckle landing on bone, can cause all kinds of injuries (and worse) when a punch lands in the worst possible spot. In fact, the first time I ever broke my hand was punching Ryan Eccles (Eccy) because he'd taken a boxing picture of Matt Mowitt off my desk. The stories in this chapter are just what happened at the time; I'm telling you the story but I'm not glorifying that violence.

As I've grown older and wiser I've learned to walk away from that kind of trouble. We've seen so many times where someone gets killed with one punch, one person's life ended and the other person's life destroyed. Anyone getting into a streetfight takes that kind of risk. It's just not worth it. The things in this chapter happened though. I've had to learn from those experiences and it's made me a better man now.

When I was 16 or 17, I used to start going out down town. Tommy Bradley, rest in peace, was working the door on the Stone House in the city centre. He used to box at Brendan's, so we knew each other and he'd always let me in. He'd tell me 'don't be getting in no trouble in here' because I was underage. That was the first ever bar I'd gone in. This bloke came up to me and kicked me up the arse. I thought 'cheeky get'. I might end up having to stick up for myself here, but I just walked away on this occasion.

Another night, I was out with Carl Wild and Joe Woodhouse. It was the first weekend back from the Army. We were stood outside the Kingdom, waiting in line for a kebab. This kid in front, about our age, started taking the mick out of someone in front of him. I don't like bullies, I never have, so I said sommat to him. He turned round, said sommat back, and walked off. Next minute, these blokes in their mid-20s started walking over - and they were a lot bigger than us. What they didn't know was that our business was fighting. One of them, I saw out of the corner of my eye swing for me and I managed to roll out of the way.

The others were going for Carl and Joe. The biggest one came over to me. I threw a left hook, and he was straight down and out - my first ever knockout on the street. There were grown men, proper gangster-style, coming up and giving me respect for that punch. That made me feel invincible: I thought I'll never let anyone mess with me like that guy who'd kicked me up the arse. Later on in life, I'd ended up working the doors with Tommy Bradley. We had some right times together, and he taught me not to back down from anyone. As if that was a lesson I needed to learn.

Then there was Treacle's stag do. Me & Joe Elfidh (who later turned pro, and lost to Curtis in his last fight) were the only lads from boxing team to go down. We stayed in a hotel in Cardiff with Treacle's cockney civvy mates: Billy Fields and Rick. Walking round Cardiff, we met them. Owt I said, one of Treacle's mates who I didn't know took t'piss. After a while it got too much. Even Treacle told him to calm down, but he didn't stop. It wa' proper doing my head in. There was more alcohol, more mick-taking. So when we were downstairs in this bar, I did what I used to do back at the Army when we went out around Aldershot: I always used to fizz bottles up and spray them. I sprayed Corona and proper caught Treacle's mate with it. He overreacted by pouring a full pint over my head. I threw a reyt right hand and split his lip, just below his nose.

Treacle told me: 'Ross, you better get out of here'. He knew his other civvy mates were there and he was probably right: it was best that I left.

I got a tap on the shoulder from a lad called Chad. He was just a guy that recognised me 'cos he was going out with a lass from Deepcar. He was in the Army too and just happened to be on his mate's stag do at the time. You couldn't have wrote it. We ended up going out on their stag do instead, having a great night on a stag do for some guy I've never met before or since. So me and Joe had to sneak out the back. We got a phone call from Treacle. The guy I'd punched wanted to do me in. I later heard that he waited outside the barracks for me with a knife.

A lot of my fights were with my Army Boxing Team mates. One of them really stands out though, it was a proper brawl. I'd come back from the Army Boxing team, having been down there for a year and a half in Aldershot. Because I'd won the Combined Services boxing title, they didn't send me back to my regiment. They used to look after us like that - top sportspeople are an asset to the Army, they knew it, and they looked after us.

I hadn't seen anyone from my battalion since January 2004 when I flew back from Cyprus. After succeeding, I'd gone back to receive my battalion colours. It was a great day with parades and all the usual pomp and circumstance associated with military ceremony. I was with the 2nd battalion light infantry, the first English regiment to be posted to Scotland and it was stationed in Edinburgh.

Naturally, seeing everyone for the first time in a long time, it was time to go out and celebrate - Army style. We went to Edwards' Bar in Edinburgh, and I was a few drinks into a session with 'Nobby' 'Gleasey' and 'Toddy'. At the time I was drinking vodka and Red Bull. Gives you wings and a headache. It was a great time until some Scottish lads came in with some lasses, and I put my drink down next to me on the side. We were an English unit in Scotland, so you'd often find that the civvies would try to cause trouble with the squaddies. One of the Scottish lads came over, and started downing my drink. "That's my drink!", I said. "No it in't", he replied. His lass came up to me, pushing me and everything. I wouldn't hit a girl of course, and I didn't know how else to react when she was being so aggressive towards me.

I don't know why, probably because I'd had a few drinks and it was funny, but I kissed her on the head instead. That's when all hell broke loose. Out of the corner of my eye, I saw a pitcher of beer coming towards me. I'm not a champion boxer for nothing, I know how to avoid punches and apparently I know how to avoid pitchers of beer too. I ducked, rolling out of the way of the flying pitcher with the skill of a proper boxer. Toddy wasn't so quick, and it hit him right in the face. There were different groups of us squaddies out, but we all stuck together. You don't always know everyone by name but you recognise the faces and you know that they're in your regiment.

There were glasses and punches flying everywhere. Toddy's face was pouring with blood, split from one side of his lip up to the opposite cheek, going round his face - not that you'd have been able to see it at the time, with that amount of blood everywhere. He's still got the scar to prove it, and he's not going to forget 43 stitches in a hurry. We found ourselves fighting to defend ourselves, other civvies piled in on the other side, other squaddies joining in to back up their regiment, and the bouncers trying to keep the peace by piling in on us.

We did a fighting withdrawal from Edwards' Bar. We needed to call an ambulance for Toddy, who was in a right mess. The other squaddies were presumably still in the bar in the middle of the melee, but it was all happening so fast. There were just the four of us trying to get away. A gang of maybe 20 or more of them were following us, but we kept pushing them back and eventually managed to phone the ambulance. If I hadn't seen that pitcher coming, it would've been me. They say proper mates in the Army would take a bullet for you, but Toddy took a pitcher for me.

Then there was the time I was outside a club called the Niche in Sheffield, and this lass I was going out with at the time got a bit lippy to someone and slapped him across the face. He pushed her back, so I had no choice to defend her and say something to him. It lead to a few words back and forwards before he threatened to "fucking knock me out". He was a big, big man but nobody fucking knocks me out; I gave him a big right hand, and he went down. We ended up scuffling on the floor as the police turned up.

When they pulled us apart, they yanked me up by the arm. That was the first time that my shoulder popped out. We both got arrested, but because of my injuries they took me up to the Northern General Hospital. They popped my arm back in, and I was in a sling for a few weeks. That all happened at the end of 2007, and I was due to box in February 2008. It was a race against time for my recovery. In hindsight, I'd have been better to postpone the fight, but if you haven't figured it out yet, I'm not one to back down from anything. I rushed my recovery a bit quicker than I should have.

My opponent was a journeyman, Abdul Mghrbel, with a fairly unimpressive 4-13-2 record. We were fighting at Don Valley Stadium. I picked him off in the first round, controlling the fight with my jab. There was no contest really, I was just a better fighter than he was. I got back to my corner at the end of the first round, and Glyn told me to step it up: "Let's go to work now". In the second round, I started throwing a few shots. I threw my big overarm right, the shot I teach people to throw now, but it popped my arm straight out of the socket. My right arm dropped immediately. I erupted in pain, but I was still in a fight. I kept my left hand up and kept throwing my jab, thinking I could beat this guy with one hand. The crowd started yelling at me to 'Stop showboating'. They didn't realise what had happened.

Glyn and the referee realised there was something up. The referee asked me what's wrong, and seeing that I couldn't raise my right arm, he thought I couldn't defend myself - so I was 'in no position to continue', and the fight was waved off. Injuries are harsh for a professional boxer in more ways than one. Now whenever anyone looks me up on BoxRec, they wonder how I managed to get TKO'd in the second round by a journeyman who'd only ever won four fights. They probably think I've got a glass chin or something, but actually I've got a titanium shoulder.

They rushed me down to the Northern General. As Glyn was driving me to the hospital, we had to go along the speed bumps along Fir Vale. At every speed bump I was screaming. It must have been a nerve, the pain was so horrendous. At the hospital, they put my arm back in but there was still a lot of damage.

At the time I was sponsored by Otter Telecom (who also sponsored Ricky Hatton. Their owners Martin Massey and Jason Barker always made sure that I was properly looked after). Otter were incredible. They paid for me to go down to the Spire Bushy hospital in Watford and have the operation I needed privately. The surgeon described it as the 'hammock' that holds my bone in having torn, so he had to repair all the ligaments.

He promised me that if I followed everything to the letter with my recovery, I'd be fine and it'd never come back out again. This time, I was determined not to rush to recover. I did all the physio correctly, completely by the book.

Trouble seemed to follow me everywhere though, even when I really wanted to avoid it. You'd have to laugh at some of the injuries if it weren't for the effect they had on my career. I remember January 11, 2011. Me and Nicola had got engaged at the Christmas just before. My parents were meeting hers for the first time at the La Luna restaurant on Ecclesall Road South in Sheffield, which was our favourite restaurant at that time. Both families were there: My mum and dad, my sister and her boyfriend, Nicola's mum, dad, brother and his wife. They met up, we all had a drink and a lot of laughs. Nicola's sister-in-law had some kind of work party, so we all ended up on West Street in Players' Bar. I've still no idea why we took my mum and dad there.

The usual happened. Some guy who wanted to cause a scene banged into me with his drinks. 'Watch out mate', I said. 'What the fuck you gonna do about it?' he replied. After a few more cross words were exchanged, he started punching. It turned into a full-blown fight. Some of the women there started trying to fight with Nicola and my sister. Don't get me wrong, they could hold their own anywhere. The bouncers dragged us out. Nicola, my mum and the bouncer Danny dragged me, and managed to get me out of the way. Danny kept telling me "listen, just keep out of the way", holding me. He asked "Have you calmed down Ross?". I replied "yeah", and he let me go.

That would have been the end of it, except that my sister told me "them lads are fighting with my dad". Danny said "No, you're not going". I sprinted down West Street, the bouncer chasing me, and me trying to get to the lads before the bouncer got to me. Running away from him, a few drinks inside me, I looked back over my shoulder to check that Danny wasn't gaining on me. Whilst looking back towards him, I wasn't watching what was in front of me. I ran straight into a parked car. One of my other mates, watching from a distance, said it was just like watching something from a cartoon. I'd later find out that the cruciate ligament (ACL) on my knee had snapped.

I stumbled back, drunk, to my apartment which was just around the corner. When I woke up, the pain was excruciating. Nicola took me down to the Northern General. The pain was bad enough already, but it got worse: on the trollies you're meant to pull, she pushed. This time it was a full ACL reconstruction of the right leg that was needed. Whilst that was recovering, my left leg basically overcompensated for it. My left ACL had apparently had an issue a few years before, which I'd not properly realised at the time. I'd been in a club in Sheffield and seen someone I knew

- a big lad who'd got himself a bit lairy. He was what we called a 'roidhead' [on steroids] and he started to throw me about like a ragdoll. I wasn't going to back down from a challenge and said 'anyone can do that', picking the bigger guy up myself.

Unfortunately, one of his mates kicked my leg from behind and it gave way. I'd never got the results from what had happened to my left knee because I'd moved house. In the end, I had to get both left and right legs fixed.

The funniest incident though was at the time the Army used me for a recruiting poster on billboards around the country and on the side of buses. My face was on TV screens in shopping centres. Everywhere you went, you'd see the face of rifleman Ross 'The Boss' Burkinshaw. It was just the way I like it, or should I say, love it. One day, I was out down town at the Varsity with Baxter, Jockey and Ellis. This big guy kept walking over and bumping into me and my mates, trying to start a fight. I said "What you doing?" and he said "You think you're right hard you, don't you, just cos you're in the Army and you're a boxer?"

I said "I don't think I'm hard mate, I know I am - and if I finish my drink and you're not out of my way, I'm gonna knock you out pal".

He bumped me with his shoulder one more time. I put my cider and black down, threw a left hook, and he bumped into me no more. Before the police came, the bouncer had told me to go round into my friend's restaurant next door, Khan's.

Later, Andrew the bouncer came over and told us what happened. When the lad came round, the police officer asked if he could remember anything. He pointed past the police officer, saying "It's him there".

The police officer said "There's nobody there".

He insisted that "It's him on the poster".

The policeman said 'I think you've had a bad knock to the head mate, it's just a poster'. So I got away with that one!

Chapter 11

LEARNING THE ROPES

There was a lot of expectation on me as I came up to my debut at the Metrodome in Barnsley on Nov 3rd 2006. Getting a professional boxing licence isn't the easiest of things to achieve, in and of itself. My record was already pretty impressive from my Army and amateur days, so it wasn't something that would prove to be a particular problem for me. I'd won about 37 of my 55 amateur fights, was Combined Services champion and an ABA finalist in 2005. I applied for my licence, went with Glyn as my trainer and manager in front of the Central Area Board in Wakefield, and Frank Maloney was happy to promote me.

Before we go any further, I should say this. I was one of the first people interviewed about Frank when Frank became Kellie Maloney. I'm a big believer in 'live and let live' - whatever makes Frank (now Kellie) happier and more contented is nothing you'll ever hear me criticise. So throughout this book, I'm going to refer to Frank rather than Kellie because that was the name being used at the time. All the adverts at the time said 'Frank Maloney promotions'. Today, though, I'd use the name Kellie. It's no skin off my nose to use the name Kellie, and I always do when we speak on the phone. When I mention 'Frank' and not 'Kellie' here, there's no disrespect. It's just that's the name that we were using then. Frank had just taken on my mate John Fewkes, and he knew that with me being in the Army that I'd be disciplined and would work hard. For me, getting the pro licence was just a formality. Everyone has to go through the same process.

The Barnsley Metrodome was the ideal venue for my first fight. Barnsley's just down the road from Stocksbridge, where I grew up. I think I sold 185 tickets for that fight, so I'd got a proper following on the night. I wasn't going to let my mates down, I was determined to put on a show for them.

My opponent was Robert Bunford from Wales, also on his professional debut, but he didn't bring with him so many fans. I'd never met the guy before the fight, but we've got to know each other on Facebook since. He's a real, nice, honest, hard-working bloke. As he'd not fought before professionally he was something of an unknown quantity. There wasn't any footage of his pro career for me to choose not to watch. In many ways, Rob's a bit like me: he's a family man, ex-Armed Forces, raises money for charity, and suffers from depression. In other ways, such as boxing, he's not so like me. There was a bit of a gap between his skill level and mine. The papers called that fight 'Gone in 60 Seconds' because I blitzed him out of there with a first-round stoppage just a minute into the fight. It was a very positive start to my professional career; it was important to me to look that good on my debut.

The second fight of my career was all about spending a bit more time in the ring. As an amateur, we used to fight 2-minute rounds. It's 1½-minute rounds as a kid, then 2-minute rounds as a senior amateur, and 3-minute rounds as a professional. Fighting professionally includes learning to pace yourself; if you're doing 12 3-minute rounds for a title fight, that's 36 minutes of boxing, with a rest after every 3 minutes. An amateur doing three 2-minute rounds is only fighting for 6 minutes, with a rest after every 2 minutes. When you think how physically demanding boxing is, constantly moving, constantly trying to punch your opponent, hoping to hit so hard that you knock them out, it means that learning to pace yourself is crucial to cope with professional boxing. Back in the day, they used to say Frank Bruno would 'gas' during a fight - run out of steam and find it difficult to keep punching throughout a long title fight.

When someone's never boxed before, they sometimes wonder what all the fuss is about. Surely just some 2-minute rounds can't be that much? Then they come into the gym, and just getting them to shadow-box for a round or two leaves them puffing and panting. The constant movement and punching takes some doing. Sparring takes that up a notch; doing the same thing with an opponent trying to punch you for real is a whole different level. Anyone can punch a bag, but a bag's not hitting you back. Then actually in a fight, it's another step up.

My second opponent was the journeyman Delroy Spencer, and we fought at the Town Hall in Leeds. He was a journeyman in the usual way: an expert at taking punches, defending himself, staying out of the way, and not getting knocked out. He earned his money by standing up in the ring with me for 12 minutes on that occasion and giving me more experience.

Delroy certainly gave it a good go against me, and he clearly wanted to win, but there are times when a journeyman doesn't actually want to win a fight. They earn their money by giving good young fighters plenty of rounds. If a promoter sees too many wins on a journeyman's record, it might discourage them from risking their fresh, raw, young boxing talent against them until they've got a bit more experience.

There's not much more that I can say about the fight itself, at Leeds Town Hall. The ref gave it a bit closer than I'd have put it. I thought I won the fight convincingly, but for some reason he only gave the fight to me by a single point. That's just the way it goes.

On Friday 13th (yes, I know, 13 is my lucky number) July 2007, I was due to return to the Barnsley Metrodome to fight the durable Bulgarian Yordan Vasilev. I'll often talk about how important preparation is for a fight, and I'd thought that the training camp had gone well. Every so often, you'll hear the 'fire alarm goes off at 4am at team hotel' excuse when a football team loses a match. What happened the night before my third fight was a little more bizarre.

When I say that I don't look for trouble, but trouble has a way of finding me, this is the kind of thing I mean. I was at home, asleep, hoping to get the much-needed and elusive good night's sleep that makes such a difference before a fight. Being physically alert is important. My sleep was interrupted by a loud banging on the door. I woke up to find a man covered in blood, who'd been a victim of a machete attack. I used my Army training, remained calm, and delivered first aid. His attacker was arrested, he went off to hospital, and I went back to sleep. A couple of hours later, the door went again. This time, it was the police - asking why he'd come to my house and why I'd given him first aid. I didn't know him, but Becky, the girl I was living with at the time, did. I've later met the lad, and he thanked me for helping him out. The Sheffield Star even ran a nice piece on it, and I made sure to ask them to include the fact that I was a serving soldier at the time. That's where I'd learned my first aid, of course.

To be fair, the night before the fight was more eventful than the fight itself. Yordan was a tough, pressure fighter who came out steaming. I managed to push him back, caught him with a sweet left hook to the body in the third round, and that was the end of my night. I'd never landed a body shot like it before - they had to get the paramedics into the ring with oxygen for him. I went 3-0, saw my mate Fewkes go 15-0, and that wasit.

Next, I found myself fighting against Faycal Messaoudene. It felt like a proper homecoming, fighting in Sheffield for the first time at Don Valley Stadium. It wasn't supposed to be an easy fight for me. At the time I fought him, he was a young professional trying to make his way. We were both in our fourth fights; I was 3-0 and he was 2-1.

This time, though, I was facing a young, hungry boxer who knew his way around the ring. He was a tall fighter for his weight, like myself. People said that he looked a bit like a mirror image of me. I believe he'd been a former kick-boxing champion.

Look him up today, and you'd say that his record's not much to look at. But he's faced some real quality opposition in his career. He took Ryan Burnett the full distance. He's fought people like Scott Quigg, Reece Belotti, Jeremy Parodi - and, of course, Ross 'The Boss' Burkinshaw. I took a comfortable points win, and moved to 4-0. By this time, at the age of 21, I'd started to build something of a reputation for myself. Boxing commentators started taking a more serious look at me, seeing a young lad with ability and potential coming through the ranks (the boxing ones,

Ross Burkinshaw v Feycal Messaoudene

not the Army ones - due to my boxing, I never got promoted. In the RLC you'd get an instant promotion if you won the Combined Services and boxed in the ABA finals. I'd have had to do an NCO cadre to get a promotion, which I never really had the time to do).

It was time for me to step up, so my next fight would be my first six-rounder against Shaun Doherty. It was a tough fight, on a fantastic bill. I was on the undercard of Carl Johanneson against Michael Gomez. Howard Foster is an amazing ref, but for some reason he seemed to have taken leave of his senses on that night. After I'd knocked Shaun around the ring for most of the six rounds, he gave it as a 57-57 draw. Being fair to the lad, he gave it a good go and it was a tough fight. He'd weighed in heavier than me on the night, and he was much stronger and more powerful than I was expecting. That made it my favourite kind of fight - a war. I have to confess that I did get knocked down in the fight for the first time in my career, so one round would have gone 10-8 against me. But it wasn't just me saying that I'd clearly won it despite the knockdown. I was still unbeaten, but the perfect record had gone. I always wanted to win as an amateur, but I didn't really mind so much if I lost because it was a stepping-stone to turning professional. Giving up that draw as pro really bothered me; it was now on my record for all time for everyone to see. That felt harsh, because the vast majority of boxing fans and those in the know would have given me that decision. I had to take the result on the chin, dust myself off, and come back stronger.

Why do you think I've called my autobiography Soldier On?

Chapter 12

HEARTBREAK

When I was a kid, I remember watching a documentary on TV about the gangs in Sheffield including the Mooney gang. My dad had a book about them as well. I was really into this programme and learning about them. I don't quite know why; these things happen in life - we can never quite say why one little thing fascinates us so much, when someone else might not even give it a second thought.

Then one of those great coincidences in life happened. It was in August 2006, when I'd just turned professional as a boxer, moving from the barracks and the Army Boxing Team back to civilian life (but still, of course, in the Army). The girl I met was a truly lovely person, one of life's free spirits. Her name was Rebecca Mooney - the great-granddaughter of one of the Mooney gang from all those years ago. She really lived her life to the full. As a young lad just turning 20, meeting a woman of 25 who I got on with so well, things really felt right. I started to get to know her kids, Chloe (who was around 7 at the time) and her younger brother Kallum. I've always been a family man at heart, so it wasn't just that I was dating Becky: I think if you're committed to a relationship, you're committed to their family too.

Becky was a very different person to me; she's still a friend to this day and I don't regret a minute of the time that I spent with her. Sure, we eventually split up, but I'm not one for hating an ex. Just because a relationship doesn't last forever doesn't mean that you have to think negatively about someone. No, I enjoyed Becky's company and I hope I always will be friends with her.

In the November, we went on holiday together to Gran Canaria. Whilst we'd been away, Chloe had been ill - but we didn't know how bad it was until we'd got home, and Chloe fainted. Something just seemed wrong, and I remember rushing her to the children's hospital. I was worrying, but maybe no more than you worry about anyone who's ill. But then the diagnosis hit with a chill: she had a medulloblastoma tumour the size of a satsuma on her brain.

The surgeons operated quickly, and told us that it had been a success. They'd got the tumour out so we hoped that everything was going to be okay: a major scare, but nothing permanent. Chloe had to stay in hospital for more tests, but we just hoped that the worst was over.

That, sadly, turned out not to be the case. Particles of the tumour had gone into Chloe's spinal fluid. It became clear just how serious it actually was: the cancer was spreading into her spine and into her brain. In a situation like this, you find yourself rallying around to do everything that needs to be done: the school runs with Kallum, finding accommodation close to the hospital. The charities were amazing: in particular, we'd been allowed to stay in the Ronald McDonald rooms. That at least minimised the travel backwards and forwards. We'd spend as much time as we possibly could with Chloe. Money trouble soon developed: living away from home, spending money every night on food because you couldn't waste the time of going home and cooking. My 2L Astra SRI? Too expensive, especially for the fuel costs; we traded it in for a Peugeot 206 in order to make ends meet.

I was doing a bit on the side as a doorman round this time. Not ideal, taking another job at the same time as being a serving soldier and professional boxer, but I did what had to be done. More things to juggle.

I didn't have time back then to process my emotions, to figure out all of the feelings that were going through my head. I was hurting so much inside, but for every moment that I hurt, I knew that the pain I was bottling up could not possibly compare to what Becky was going through. I was only 20; I'd not got the life experience. At times like that, the emotion gets buried deep down inside. Those are the times in life when you just have to put your own feelings on hold and look out for other people.

More anxious weeks passed. In December, a ray of hope - perhaps; they let Chloe out of hospital for Christmas Day. But it was short-lived; she took a funny turn and was back in hospital on Boxing Day. We saw in the New Year with her family all by her bedside in the intensive care unit. We got moved into a house, Pact House, which was a place where families can live in order to be close to the children's hospital. Then, not long after that, we got the phone call I'd been dreading. It was from the hospital, telling us to get there as quickly as we could. We feared the worst, and so Becky rushed to the hospital first. I had to sort

Kallum with a babysitter before rushing down to hospital to be with Chloe. I couldn't imagine the thought of not being there in time. I remember thinking 'I don't mind, even if I crash, as long as Chloe survives'. My car hit a bollard; I crashed. Amazingly, I was completely unharmed. Chloe made it through the night.

Tragically, though, it wasn't long before Chloe passed away. The vicar christened her whilst she was in hospital; I became her Godfather and one of Becky's friends was the Godmother. All we could do was be there for her until April, when she died.

Even in that grief, it was important to hold myself together as much as I could. For Becky. For Kallum. The funeral was held at St. John's Church in Deepcar. I'd always gone there when I was growing up though I'm not religious, one bit. It felt a bit like our family church. My mum and dad had got married there before I was born, and I'd gone to the local C of E school growing up so we'd spent plenty of time at that church.

That day, though, was different. There was a white horse-drawn carriage. I was one of the coffin-bearers carrying the coffin in to the church. Chloe will always have a special place in my heart. It felt so awful, so unfair, so devastating what had happened to her. It was so difficult, to be there in the right way for Becky and for Kallum. How do you have all the answers to the tough questions? Why? Why did something like this happen?

What could I possibly say to Becky? Nobody, and I mean nobody, can find the right words to say to make it all okay again. It isn't. The passage of time can ease some of the pain, but it doesn't take it away.

I lost another close friend whilst all this was going on. The first time that I got to spend a night out, away from the hospital, Chloe's dad was at the hospital instead. I went out drinking with some mates in Hillsborough and then went into Stocksbridge.

We saw this grey Astra, and it had clearly just been in a horrible accident. I thought 'that's Helen's car'. Helen was a big girl, about 18 stone. She always used to mess about, saying that I was her 'little brother'. She'd actually been adopted and we were great friends. We phoned the fire brigade and an ambulance straight away, but only the ambulance arrived.

Tony Button was the guy who was out with me, and the paramedics had to ask us to help to get her out of the car. We had to snap the door back to get in, and the paramedics got the back brace in. We got her on the stretcher, and I phoned Becky straight away, telling her 'I think Helen's dead'.

They pronounced her dead on arrival at the hospital, but I knew that she was dead in my arms.

All this was going on whilst I was in my early 20s, just at the start of my career. There aren't any words I can use to explain the grief I felt: losing Chloe, losing Helen, two people I loved dearly in very different ways, so close in time to each other.

Life can be so cruel at times.

After me and Becky split, I ended up with this girl called Emily who was like a Barbie doll. If you know that song by Mike Skinner & The Streets, that girl was really fit but didn't she just know it!

I was getting on with Emily really well, and it seemed that she was always staying round at the flat that I had. Even so, it felt a bit like I was always the one expected to do all the chasing. We'd been on holiday together and everything, but I got the same sixth sense - that feeling that something just wasn't right. If there's one thing I've learned, it's 'always follow your gut'. I later found out that she was cheating on me.

It wasn't the first time either that I'd been cheated on. Down at the Army Boxing Team, I'd been going out with this lass who I'd known from school. I'm not even going to mention her name, she's not worth it. While I was in Aldershot, I phoned her up. She was in the local pub where she worked. I could tell that there was something wrong - like I said, I've always had a bit of a sixth sense with some things.

She phoned me when she was leaving, and she was walking on with a couple of my friends and a few of her mates. I couldn't get hold of her later on that night.

I didn't think too much more of it until a few weeks later, when her mum warned me off her. I was wondering why a mum would be warning me about her own daughter, and trying to work out why. It turned out that she'd slept with my mate in her mum's bed. Her mum knew 'cos they'd bust one of the slats on the bed.

At the time, I fell out with my mate - and rightly so. Now, though, I see it as a blessing in disguise. At least things didn't end up getting too serious with that girl. I've forgiven my mate for it, although of course I can't ever truly forget.

With everything that had gone on, I started to find it harder and harder to trust people that I was with. I'd known so many girls to be cheating on their partners that I was always getting afraid that it would happen in any relationship.

Becky was different. She was an absolutely amazing person. I'm so glad that we spent the time together that we did, in spite of everything. She might not have been my soulmate, but she's one of the best people I've ever known in my life. What we went through was incredibly tough, but she'll always be my friend. I'm just pleased that she's moved on and found happiness with the person who's right for her.

Chapter 13

SLAYING THE DRAGON

"Shoot for the moon - because even if you miss,
you'll be amongst the stars"

If there's one thing I'd wanted since I was a kid, it was to win titles. I wasn't going to be the kid who carried Clinton's belts, kids were going to want to carry *my* belts into the ring. My first title fight opportunity came totally out of the blue. I got a call from Frank Maloney [now Kellie] giving me the chance to fight for the English title. I was proper buzzing about it.

The fight was due to take place on St. George's Day, April 23rd 2009. To me that was just destiny. I'm a proper patriot. I love my country, I love the Royal Family and everything. I just hate it when I see people doing our country down. In boxing, I always wanted to be the best. I want my country to be the best and you don't achieve that by knocking it. It's a bit like family: your family don't always get everything right, but you love them and you're proud of them whenever they do something that's good. Fighting on St. George's Day made it more special for me. That title was coming back with me, no matter what. I'll never forget that date either because I've got the tattoo to make sure I remember it for the rest of my life. My mate Steve Bodell did the tattoo for me.

My training camp for that fight was a bit different, because it was the first time I'd headlined the bill. That meant it would likely be at least 10pm by the time I got into the ring. Michael Lovett, who did my strength and conditioning, told me I needed to change my routine. I didn't want to be ready to fall asleep by the time I went out to fight, so I made sure to do something late at night every day to get my body

used to the exercise. Whether it was a late-night run or 10-12 rounds of shadowboxing with light weights, I needed to make sure I was ready for a late-night fight.

At one point, though, it looked like I was going to miss out on the title altogether. I needed to weigh in at 8 stone 3 for the fight. I woke up the morning of the weigh-in, April 22 2009, and I couldn't make the weight. I got in the sauna down at the Sheffield Hilton, and I was just bone dry. There was no sweat coming out. Back in those days, we did dieting differently. We tried to lose water weight, something that's frowned on now because it leaves you open to brain damage and all kinds of things. Boxing's not as dangerous as people think it is, but if you drain water weight, you also drain protection from the membranes around your brain - and that can take weeks to recover. If a boxer's hurt in a fight, nine times out of ten the reason's to do with making the weigh. I was getting worried when Jez Wilson came in and said "Ross, you don't even have a sweat on."

He got me to put a black binliner on, and pushed me to work hard on the treadmill. After I'd got back home and got changed, Fewky picked me up with my mate Scott Roberts because Glyn couldn't come to London till later that night and we travelled down in

Scott's 1-series. Fewky said I kept talking to him, rambling, answering questions that he didn't even ask. He said later that I must have been hallucinating, but he just went along with what I was saying because he didn't want to worry me. It was brutal but I managed to get under 8 stone 3 by a whisker. When I say it was by a whisker, I mean it! I eventually weighed in at 8 stone 2½.

That was the day before the fight, though, and I felt right as rain and ready to fight on the night. I was down to box Mike 'Robbo' Robinson, a very tough fighter who I'd drawn to once before. The fight was on Frank Maloney's show at the Troxy in London, called 'The Slayers', and it was going to raise money for the Army Benevolent Fund.

It was the first time that I'd really noticed celebrities coming to watch me fight. Christopher Ellison, the actor who played DCI Burnside from The Bill, was there. He was a really big name at the time. There were big boxing names present, including Michael Watson MBE. Terry Marsh was there too, but I didn't find that out until later. As I walked out from the changing rooms upstairs, someone from the British Boxing Board of Control was carrying the English belt. Someone from Robinson's team said "That's going home with us tonight". I turned to Glyn and Fewky and said "Not a chance". I felt I was destined to win that night - I'd kept finding little white feathers everywhere I'd been, something I'd always thought was lucky. Friends, family and fans had made the journey down to London to watch me. One of them, Jamie Vardy, you might know because he went on to play for England at the last football World Cup. I wasn't able to choose my entrance music for the fight, because Frank had arranged for a singer

(Jill Daniels) from the Army to sing me into the ring. She did a cracking job of it too. As a serving soldier in the Rifles, I came into the ring wearing my green camouflage jacket and beret.

After my injury against Mghrebel, I'd come back with a routine four-rounder against Mike Holloway who I'd knocked out. The fight itself against Holloway had been pretty straightforward, a bit of a mismatch really. In fact, there was more fighting afterwards - there was a bit of a riot in the crowd. A lot of my fans were Sheffield Wednesday supporters, and his fans were mainly from Leeds, leading to tension between his fans and mine.

My second fight back had been against the same Mike Robinson. I'd fought him over four rounds, and it had been given as a draw. I had to fight him again, just six weeks later, for the English title. The fight for the English title was over ten rounds though. He was undefeated, but he'd never been beyond six rounds before - and that had been against a journeyman on his debut. Come to think of it, I'd never gone beyond six rounds either! This was going to be a bit more about endurance and I thought a longer fight would suit me.

My trainers thought the opening few rounds were fairly even. In my corner, Glyn started to shout across to him 'Are you tired, Mike?' and kept telling me that my opponent looked tired. It was a proper fight, blood coming out of my nose as well as his. But if there's one thing that I had, it was the heart to dig deep. I caught him with a body shot which forced him to take a knee. I thought 'I can do this here. I can stop him', and jumped on him again. I forced him down a second time, throwing a powerful combination. Again, he beat the count - but only just. It wasn't long before Ian-John Lewis stepped in…

…And The New!

The words I'd dreamed of hearing, ever since I was a boy. I was now the English Super-Flyweight champion, well on the road to success. As a young lad of 22, it was a dream come true. Happy St. George's Day; I'd slayed the dragon!

Suddenly, everyone wanted to spend more time with Ross The Boss. I was invited to dine with royalty at the Rifles Salamanca Day Awards Dinner. This was a huge event; it was something that nobody would ever normally dream of inviting a mere Private to. If you weren't a Captain or above, you had very little chance of being allowed to attend this prestigious black-tie event. They even paid for me to be put up in the Cumberland Hotel.

Prince Phillip was in attendance; Princess Alexandra was on my table. She was very interested in my story and very attentive to

Salamanca Dinner Invitation

whatever I was saying. I knew my Ps and Qs; Yes Ma'am, No Ma'm. She asked me why I boxed; I told her that I loved it and I'd been doing it since I was just 8 years old. Isn't it very barbaric? No; in fact, it changes people's lives. It's changed mine - the structure, the discipline, taking people who would otherwise be street fighters and giving them a purpose and a passion. I didn't have a fight coming up at the time. Having been dieting for months, I would easily get full up and couldn't have much more. She very kindly said that I should have her dessert. I wasn't used to eating a 3-course meal any more; I was so full but felt obliged. Who could say No Ma'am to royalty?

"St. George's Day, Champion of England 2009". That's what my tattoo says.

Chapter 14

I AM NOT THE REFEREE

"Everyone has bad days and evereyone has bad moments, but it's how you handle them that matters most. Even champions lose rounds."

Having won the English title, the next obvious step was to challenge for the British super-flyweight crown. It was up at the Seaburn Centre in Sunderland, and I was topping the bill

Calm before the storm

again. This time the bout would be shown on Sky TV, back in the days before Eddie Hearn took over pretty much everything that's ever shown on Sky Sports. A lot of the names on my undercard were ones we've already mentioned: journeymen Delroy Spencer and Kristian Laight were putting Kyle King and Chris Mullen through their paces, whilst Tony Jeffries was continuing his short but undefeated career. Jon-Lewis Dickinson, who'd later win a Lonsdale Belt and the Commonwealth cruiserweight title, was also notching up some wins at the start of his career.

I was due to face the tricky southpaw boxer Lee Haskins. Now don't get me wrong, all southpaw boxers are tricky in one way. Fighting against a southpaw is different - all the angles are wrong. Because there are fewer southpaw boxers, they get plenty of sparring experience against orthodox fighters but orthodox fighters get much less experience fighting against southpaws. It's the same principle in most sports: facing a left-arm bowler in cricket, playing tennis against a left-hander - they're used to coming up against people like you, but you're not quite so used to fighting them.

Lee Haskins was the first southpaw that I'd faced as a professional, and challenging for a British title was a big step up. Haskins had an 18-2 record. He'd go on to challenge for a world title years later, and throughout his career he never lost a non-title fight. Everyone, including Kell Brook, thought that his style would be ideal for me to face in a different way. His hands-down boxing style, relying upon speed in the Brendan Ingle mould, was what you expected of a lot of Sheffield fighters. They just assumed that this was something I was used to facing in sparring, but that wasn't really the case. I'd done my sparring at Glyn's gym, and his fighters fought in a very different style to that. Haskins was actually very different to what I was used to facing. This was never going to be an easy fight. I could have done with sparring with people who weren't at my gym; at Glyn's everything was kept under one roof. That was good in one way because we were a close-knit team but we rarely went to other gyms to spar, and others very rarely came to spar with us. When I was with Ryan later in my career, I sparred with Kal Yafai, Jerome Wilson, Curtis Woodhouse, Paul Butler, Muheeb Fazeldin and many others. I blacked Curtis Woodhouse's eye the week before his British title - one of the reasons that boxers don't tend to spar so close to a fight. With Ryan, you'd travel all over the place to get more sparring. I preferred Ryan's approach with that because it got you used to so many more different styles and techniques.

Sunderland was an odd choice of venue for us to be fighting. I'm from Sheffield, and Lee's from Bristol. Plenty of my fans made the trip up the A19 to watch me, as you'd expect. I always did that in boxing. I sold tickets for my fights. If you don't sell tickets as a boxer, you don't really make any money unless you're topping the bill and on television. It's all about the money in the end. Even in some of my first professional fights, I took so many fans with me that they didn't mess around with my timings. Some young boxers would find their fight being the 'floater'. That meant they'd have to be ready to go out and box whenever there was a gap in the schedule, for example if a 12-round fight was stopped because of a clash of heads in round 1.

If things were running behind schedule on a big card, they might not get into the ring until midnight - by which time most people would have gone home, everyone would be bored and the venue would be almost empty. If they weren't the floater, they'd be the first fight on - before the TV cameras were filming, and whilst most of the fans either hadn't arrived or were sitting in the bar. They didn't get that atmosphere right from the first fight. With my fights, even on my debut I'd sold enough tickets to justify being higher up the bill. Want to make it as a young professional boxer? Make sure people want to come along and watch you. Be exciting. Money talks.

"I am the referee"

Whenever Ian-John Lewis is refereeing a fight, that's his catchphrase. He's a respected ref, and he says that to fighters before each fight to remind us that he's in charge, something he was advised to do when he started out so that he'd command respect. He stuck with it.

Before the fight, Ian-John Lewis came into the dressing room and told me "If you're taking too many shots, show me you that know where you are by taking a knee". I took that too literally, as it would later turn out.

Haskins was a quality boxer. The bell sounded for the start of round 1, and it was time to get to work. Jason 'Bad Boy' Barker was another professional, and also one of my sponsors. He said that I needed to take the fight to Haskins, to have a war, to give him no room whatsoever to move. Glyn, though, gave me a different game plan: to sit back for the first few rounds, and find out what he had to offer. He wanted me to box like I'd done on the Army team. In the end I followed Glyn's advice, but Haskins was so fast and elusive that I was starting to get madder and madder. Another tip for young boxers - don't get mad, don't get angry, don't get overconfident, just relax and do your thing. When you're relaxed, focusing on your breathing, you box better than when you get yourself all flustered.

In the fourth round, I started getting caught with some heavy punches. The shots were coming in so fast that I didn't want the referee to think that I couldn't defend myself. I thought I'd better take a knee, just like he'd said in the dressing room. I didn't want the fight to be called off. I took the knee, and he caught me with another shot just as I went down onto one knee. I waited for the count, ready to get back up, change plans, and go to war. Ian-John Lewis just waved the fight off. I wasn't expecting that to happen.

I was fucking devastated.

Chapter 15

THE BOSS'S BOSS

After the Haskins fight, I needed to get back to winning ways. Over the next year, I had three more professional fights and won them all fairly comfortably. I beat Anwar Alfadli, Daniel Thorpe and Delroy Spencer (again) as Glyn did some work developing my technique.

Glyn advising me during Thorpe fight

I'd already won the English title at super-flyweight; now, after making the step up to bantamweight, I'd be fighting to win the title at a second weight. Craig Lyon would be my opponent. In early August of 2010, I was at Glyn's gym when we got a call saying that Phil Wood had left his boxing gym in the building.

Phil used to train at Glyn's gym before he got his own place. The landlord wondered whether Glyn wanted to buy any equipment.

We went down to the gym on Earsham Street in Pittsmoor, near a pub called the Royal Oak. It needed some work doing, but it was a boxing gym - and a gym's a gym. Rather than buying anything, I asked Glyn whether it would be okay for me to set this up as my own gym. I loved personal training and often used to cover Glyn's classes whilst he was away. Glyn and the landlord both agreed, so I opened it on the week of my 24th birthday. To start with, I was just running mixed Boxercise classes and some women's only classes.

One of the girls, Nicola, who came into the gym used to turn up with her two young boys and a couple of friends. She'd got two plaits in her really long hair. She started doing circuit classes, and kept on turning up on a regular basis. She was really helpful, printing off things like my timetables - and daft things, like bringing me in Haribo sweets 'cos she knew I liked them. I really took to her.

At the time I was focused on training for my fight against Craig Lyon, which I knew would be a tough one. By this time, I'd switched promoters: Ricky Hatton was now promoting me. A guy we knew as Blobby (his mum ran the Royal Oak) was really good at taking people on the pads; he'd learned the skill from Reagan Denton during his time in prison. It wasn't easy for me to run my gym and head over to Glyn's at the same time to train, so Blobby would often take me on the pads leading up to the fight in October 2010. At the time, I'd bounced back from my defeat to Haskins with three wins on the trot. I was feeling good, and looking forward to another tough test.

Having seen me train, Nicola decided to buy a ticket to watch me fight. We'd kind-of spoken about maybe going on a date, but hadn't really taken it much further than that and it was a bit awkward 'cos I was sort-of still seeing another girl at the time. I remember I'd promised Nicola that I'd buy her a ticket, but she insisted on paying her own way. It was different - most girls would take me up on anything I offered, but Nicola wasn't like that at all. My grandad Brian went to that fight, which was a big thing for me because he didn't get to many of my fights. He'd fallen out with my mum, but this time my mum and dad were away. Kath and Russ, my aunt and uncle, gave him a lift. I was absolutely made up that he was there to see me.

It was a great boxing bill up in Bolton, with Foster against Kirakosyan, and Anthony Crolla against Andy Morris. On our undercard, Adam Etches was making his debut - another boxer who'd go on to make a name for himself.

The fight itself was a bit less dramatic. He caught me with a big right hand in the first round and put me down. It was the worst pain I'd had in the boxing ring, at least the worst that had been caused by a punch. My face was swelling up all down below my jaw, and we thought that I'd fractured it. Naturally, I got up and continued boxing. We had a bit of a war, and I started to get myself back into the fight. The trouble was, the injury was only going to get worse if I carried on. Glyn said he was going to pull me out of the fight; I argued with him, as you do, but it was totally the right decision. I retired on my stool at the end of the 5th round.

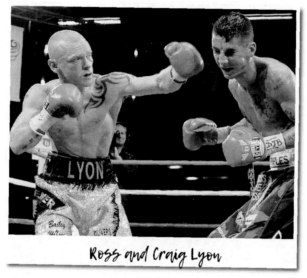

Ross and Craig Lyon

I travelled back across to Sheffield on the evening with a really good mate, Carl Betts, who was living with me at the time. We headed straight for Butler's Balti House, owned by my friend Saj. I sat down, crying into my curry. Not properly crying, of course, I just felt like that. The phone rang, and it was Nicola. She asked me how I felt, and told me that she wanted to come down and see me. Carl insisted: 'Don't let her see you like this'. She said that she just wanted to come and give me a hug. It was the first time that I really started to have feelings towards her. She told me that her mum and dad watched my fight on Sky Sports in Lanzarote in one of the bars, and that if I wanted a break to get my head right, I'd be welcome to go to their place. All I'd have to do would be to pay for my flights. I shrugged it off as one of those things that people say but don't mean, but the next day she phoned again and repeated the offer.

"Who am I gonna go with though?" I asked her. She'd just been made redundant that week and had no work, but she said she couldn't go because there'd be nobody to look after her kids. I said "Well I'm not bothered that you've got kids, bring them too". It all happened so fast. Two days after that devastating loss, on October 4th 2010, we got together. We booked flights on the Tuesday, flew to Lanzarote on the Thursday, and met her parents Sue and Tony and her aunt Christine on arrival. I'd say that when the Boss makes a move, the Boss moves fast, but it wasn't really like that: things just happened that way.

Ross and Nicola in Lanzarote

There I was, away in a foreign country not just with a girl I hardly knew - but with her kids and her family who I'd never met before. Everything seemed great though, getting to know each other. We hired a convertible, went out driving into the hills with the kids, already doing things in the way that a family would. They'd never really known their biological dad - Nicola told me that their biological dad literally wanted to have nothing to do with them. With her kids and her mum and dad, I felt like I was accepted into their family straight away. It just clicked, and I remember our joke at the time was when I said that 'it's like a Pot Noodle: Just add Ross'.

Everything was amazing until the Sunday night; the holiday was absolutely brilliant. Then I woke up on the Monday morning, and the phone rang. It was my sister Carla, crying her eyes out. She said that grandad had just been rushed to the hospital. I asked her what had happened, but she didn't know too much at the time so I phoned my mum to ask what had happened. She didn't know much either, just that he'd had to go to hospital. It can't have been more than half an hour later that I got another phone call from Carla. Grandad Brian had passed away.

Now I was stuck in a foreign country, hardly really knowing Nicola at that time, and with her family who I'd known for less than a week. They really went out of their way to take care of me, and all I can say is that things just felt okay with them. I was so comfortable with Nicola and her family. I started to feel like Nicola was the girl I wanted to spend the rest of my life with. I was so sad at the time; looking back now, I'm really thankful that grandad Brian had been to my fight just a week or so before. Everything happened so fast: a rollercoaster from low to high to low in the space of just a few days. That's the story of my life.

Christmas came around; I found myself spending it at Nicola's mum and dad's. We went out on Christmas Eve in Vodka

Revolution with some of my old mates from Stocksbridge. In some kind of drunken stupor I told them how I felt about Nicola, and the words just popped out: "I think I'm gonna propose to Nicola".

Their response? "Go on, do it. The stag do'll be mega". Not entirely sure that was the best reason...

Nicola's mum picked me up later and drove me home with Nicola. When we got back to their place, her dad was busy making beef sandwiches in the kitchen and potatoes. Nicola and her mum were in the living room, and even in my somewhat drunken state, I still got a little bit shy. I asked him:

"Tony, can I?"

"Can you what?", he said, somewhat confused.

"Can I?", I repeated, as though that was going to clear things up in some way.

"Can you what?", he asked again.

Finally, I found the words: "Can I ask Nicola to marry me?"

He rushed through and grabbed a bottle of champagne, saying loudly in front of Nicola: "Susan, we've got sommat to celebrate. Ross is going to ask Nicola to marry him!"

That wasn't, perhaps, exactly how I'd have wanted the proposal to start. I looked at Nicola… "Will you then?"

She said yes. It wasn't the most romantic proposal in the world. Tony did it for me, and because I hadn't really planned and prepared the proposal, I didn't have any money. I even had to borrow a grand off Nicola to get her an engagement ring.

Ross. Nicola, Reuben and Pharrell

If the proposal wasn't romantic, we certainly planned to make up for it with the wedding. That was absolutely mega; we booked it in Varadero, Cuba, for the following May. Instead of just the traditional invitations, we put it on Facebook and told people that they'd be welcome to book on if they wanted to come to our wedding. When you're travelling halfway across the world to get married in Cuba, you don't really expect too many guests. In the end, there were 69 of us who made the journey.

Nothing's ever simple with me though. A few weeks before going to Cuba, I had a horrible pain on the left-hand side of my abdomen. I had tests at the doctors, then more tests with more doctors. I was glad to have the private healthcare through the Army. After a CT scan and an MRI, I went back for the results five days before flying out. They said they'd found a lump on my bladder. They didn't know, but it could potentially be cancerous. They wanted to book me straight in for an operation on the Monday, but I was due to be flying out on the Wednesday. I asked how long I'd be in hospital, and they told me it'd
be about 10 days. I said I couldn't, because I was flying out to Cuba to get married. They made sure that I'd book in for the operation the moment I got back.

We flew out to Cuba in mid-May, together with most of the 69 guests - minus the 10 or so from my family in Canada. My friend Joe was a photographer, so we paid for him to go in exchange for taking photos of us everywhere. There's photos of us on the plane, photos coming off the plane, photos of everyone and everything as well as the traditional wedding photos.

My mates had been right a few months earlier: the stag do was going to be mega indeed. My stag do involved taking a catamaran to another island. I was on the rum punch, getting absolutely paralytic. I'm not teetotal at the best of times. I can't remember a single thing about that, until the point where me and Dale got into a drunken play-fight. I was 9 stone; he was 18 stone. Fighting on a catamaran after a few drinks isn't the most stable thing you can do. He fell on top of me, my knee seemed to crack into the opposite direction to usual, and I hit my head into the fibreglass. There were three long splits down the side of my head. That sobered me up in a hurry, not least because 'Nicola's gonna kill me'. We got back, and they tried to hide me from Nicola.

Eventually, she found me - complete with Adidas stripes of blood across my head. We have two sets of wedding photos: the airbrushed ones of the happy couple, and the non-airbrushed photos still bearing the scars of the stag do. We got married in a beautiful ceremony, despite everything. Nicola became the Boss's Boss. Later in the same evening, we were dancing and Nicola said something that I don't want to repeat in this book. She ended up causing an argument over absolutely nothing. I should have realised at this point that maybe things weren't as great as I thought. Then she later went absolutely crazy at her father as well; maybe I should have realised that she had a bit of a split personality. She even chucked her engagement and wedding rings off into the bushes and I went scrambling for them. They say things can get a bit spicy on your wedding night, but that's not what most people have in mind! I'm always optimistic, though, so I thought everything will be alright.

My knee was absolutely killing me. We got back to England, and I headed straight to the hospital. I needed a full ACL reconstruction, which is about as much fun as it sounds. Because of the hospital's rules on preventing MRSA, I had to wait a few days before my bladder operation. Whilst in hospital for the bladder operation, my left leg started to swell. That had become infected, so it meant another operation to re-do the ACL and drain the fluid off my leg. I got back from my wedding, and ended up spending over 30 days in hospital. The vows do say 'in sickness and in health'. It seemed I was forever waiting for the 'in health' bit. I reckon they owe me that much.

Still, something just always felt right about Nicola and the kids. I joined a ready-made family; it was an adoption in reverse. It was more like the kids adopting me, than me adopting them. One time, we were out in Lanzarote on holiday and Tony took me to one side. He said there's something that Pharrell had asked him to talk to me about. Pharrell wanted to know if it'd be okay for him to call me 'dad'. His biological dad didn't have anything to do with him any more, and he'd seen the difference between us, and said that I'm ten times the dad he'll ever be. Hearing that was just the best feeling ever; a sudden feeling of happiness and joy, pride in a way. I said that I was totally okay with it, but that of course they'd have to check with Nicola. She said that I do everything a real dad should, so why not? Next time I saw him, he called me "Ross, I mean, dad". That was the last time he ever called me Ross. It was a bit different with Reuben in a way, because he couldn't really remember anything other. I was boxing pro, so I used to take Reuben to the gym with me whilst Nicola was at work and Pharrell was at school. What other lad has a boxing gym as his creche?

I remember when Pharrell asked to call me dad, Reuben was just learning to speak. I can remember it now, we had a little dinghy boat and we were pulling it round in the pool. He couldn't pronounce his 'r's yet, so he kept calling me 'Daddy Wo'. It was dad for both of them from then on. My own dad was the best; he still is. I tried to treat the kids just like my dad treated me.

Chapter 16

GIVING SOMETHING BACK

"It's nice to be important, but it's more important to be nice"

I've always wanted people to know me, to know Ross The Boss. I love it whenever someone recognises me in the street, or when I'd see so many fans coming to watch me box. It gives me a great opportunity to make a difference to other people's lives, as well. I've always believed it's important to give something back to the community; I learned that from an early age when Paul 'Silky' Jones went out of his way to help a young Ross Burkinshaw raise money to try to keep his local gym open.

The boxing community is great at doing that, in one way or another. Most professionals I know have always been willing to help out. Sometimes that's mentoring a kid who wants to grow up to be a boxer, taking them on the pads and giving up time to help them. Herol Bomber Graham used to do that for me. It might be providing sponsorship to the next generation of boxers.

Michael Lawless helped me to get sponsorship, and did so much for me over the years behind the scenes without ever really getting the kind of praise he truly deserved.

Sometimes boxers will give something back by running events for a local gym; for others, it's helping raise awareness of good causes or raising money for charities and helping them to do the work they do to make a difference to people's lives.

With all the help I've had over the years, I can't pay that back to the champs who used to give up their time for me - but I can pay it forward to other people. Coming from Stocksbridge and Deepcar, I've always been a Sheffield Wednesday fan so I've done a lot of charity work with them. After my first comeback fight, I stepped into the ring with Sheffield Wednesday's chaplain to raise money for neurocare and a charity working with families of children with tumours. It seemed appropriate after everything that had happened with Chloe.

Ross during a White Collar Boxing event

I ended up doing some work as an ambassador for Sheffield Wednesday's community projects. A lot was about inspiration and motivation: giving talks about my career, about the life of a professional sportsman, helping young people to believe in themselves to achieve their dreams. Everyone would always want to see my belts, and many times they'd get me to do presentations for community projects or even sometimes I'd do the half-time draw at some of the Owls matches. If there's one thing I can't do, it's play football. Curtis Woodhouse, my footballer-turned-boxer-turned-football manager mate, knows a bit about how to play. He was on the Blades side in the 'Reds v Blues' charity football match in 2014 to raise money for St. Luke's Hospice, and I was on the Blues team. I may be no good at football, but I could at least stop someone who was: I remember taking him out with a pretty good tackle. Just don't ask whether I got the ball or the man.

There's always someone contacting me, even now, asking for help with something. That's how I got involved with the Balls to Cancer campaign, which has really been about raising awareness. I've got a lot of very committed fans on my social media. Then, there's the constant requests - for autographs, signed photos, memorabilia and everything else. I've never had a problem with sending kids a signed photo or something, 'cos that's what boxers did for me when I was collecting signatures when I was little. Some of the letters I get are actually quite inspirational for me. It's always surprised me how easily they managed to find my address.

Those requests are easy enough to manage, but when they're asking for signed pairs of my boxing gloves for charity auctions and raffles, that's a bit different. I'm always happy to oblige, but there's a supply and demand problem here. I think they think I've got a warehouse full of old boxing gloves ready to send out. I try to do the best I can.

I've tried to help the Army Benevolent Fund and the Rifles Benevolent Fund over the years. In fact, when I won my English title back in 2009 on St. George's Day, the event was raising money for the Army Benevolent Fund.

Raising money for 3 Rifles Wristband Appeal

But of all the charities, the one I've probably done the most work with is Hallam FM Cash For Kids. The first time I heard about it I thought it seemed like a great cause. I'm a bit of a local guy, so I like local charities where the money goes to helping people in the area I know and love, the area I care the most about. The work they do with local kids helps people right here in South Yorkshire, so I got in touch and wanted to help.

Later in my career, Dave Coldwell had a team of people working

with him; one of them was Damien Harry (who we knew as Dimmi). After I'd retired, he came to see me when I was at the Gleadless gym. He wanted to start running some white collar shows with me, to put my name to them and get me to train the fighters. I agreed, on two conditions: firstly, I wanted the charity that we were supporting to be Hallam FM Cash for Kids. Secondly, I wanted to have a bigger involvement with actually putting on the shows.

I got in touch with Allan Ogle, who was managing the charity by that time, and we started to get everything in place to put on some shows. The work involved was incredible, but it's so rewarding to see it all coming together.

I'd have to train the fighters twice a week for 10 weeks leading up to the show. We'd have to source a big enough venue, organise ticketing and sort the fighters to sell their own tickets. Then there's meals for VIP tickets, dietary requests, organising everything from PA systems to paramedics to publicity and press releases, raffles, insurance, health and safety, the gear, the referee and the cornermen. There's so much involved before we even start to think about the show itself. We aimed to do four shows a year; after the first four we'd raised over £10,000.

Sometimes it's easy to forget how much of a difference the little things actually make to people's lives. When I did inspirational talks and training sessions at local schools, I didn't really think too much more about it at the time. Strangely though, since I've retired I've had loads of people come up to me in the street - or even my taxi drivers recognising me on my way home from a night out - and tell me that they remember what I said, that it's kept them out of bother.

If boxing's a family, then we need to set an example to the next generation too. Just like all my mentors helped me along the way, I want to help the next generation of boxers to understand their responsibilities so that they grow up to be the kind of people to make a difference too.

Chapter 17

YOU GOTTA GET LOW BEFORE YOU TASTE THE HIGHS

"I'm strong because I've been weak. I'm fearless because I've been afraid. I'm wise because I've been foolish."

The defeat to Craig Lyon, the bladder operation, the Adidas stripes on my face and the double operation on my ACL were plenty to worry about, so it wasn't just settling in to married life that kept me out of the ring for fully 18 months before I finally got back into action. It wasn't until the end of April 2012 before my next fight. My opponent would be the South African fighter, Michael Ramabeletsa, at Don Valley Stadium.

Everything went wrong on the night in the build-up to that fight. My phone was going off like a Christmas tree when I should have been preparing and focusing totally on the fight. I never usually answer my phone when I'm in the changing room. I normally switch it off, but for some unknown reason I'd left it on this time. I got a ping on my Blackberry Bold. I read the message; it was from Nicola. "I can't believe that slag is your ring card girl".

I asked her "What are you on about?" She told me 'that slag Lucy

Victoria' was the ring card girl.

I'd got a bit of a history with Lucy Victoria, and it all went back to before the Craig Lyon fight 18 months earlier. When I was just getting to know Nicola, I'd had a bit of a thing with Lucy Victoria. I wasn't dating Nicola by then, and I'd got a message on my Facebook saying 'you're hot' from Lucy Victoria.

Lucy was pretty well known at the time; she was the first English Playboy model in about 24 years and she used to live at Hugh Heffner's house. When I saw who it was that messaged me, believe me, I knew! Lads tend to know these things for some reason…

Being the cocky lad that I am, I simply replied "I know"

She asked "When are you taking me out on a date?"

At around that time, before I was dating Nicola (obviously), I'd arranged to go out for a meal with Nicola, to say thank you for the things she'd done. She'd been helping me with paperwork at the gym and a few other things.

So I took Lucy Victoria out on a date. We went for food, one thing led to another, and I didn't end up taking Nicola out on the Saturday. It was a bit stupid in one sense, but I wasn't dating anyone at the time.

After a week or two, Lucy Victoria wanted me to change my relationship status on Facbook to say that I was in a relationship with her. Being young and daft, I did.

Nicola kept coming to my gym; it impressed me that she just took it in her stride. After a few weeks it was getting closer to my fight. I'd started to realise that Lucy Victoria was more interested in seeking the limelight than she was in me. I didn't want a girl like that. By this time Nicola had a ticket to the fight with the twins, Simon and Ritchie Smith. So I asked Lucy Victoria not to come to my fight.

I'd made it clear to Lucy Victoria that I needed to get my head right. I've never really been that good at ending things, I'd rather just let things play out and end in their own way.

I was getting more and more keen on Nicola by this time, just because she'd not been pushy or anything like that. So when I realised she was at my fight, I said to her "I've booked a hotel, do you want to stay with me?"

She said she couldn't because she'd arranged to give Simon and Ritchie a lift home. I boxed, lost, and to be honest I didn't want to go out celebrating. I went back home to Sheffield, didn't stay in the hotel, and that's when things happened with Nicola.

As I'd been on my way down to East Midlands Airport with Nicola to go on holiday with her and get my head clear, I did what I always do. I put my heart and my life on Facebook sometimes. I changed my Facebook status to show that I was now in a relationship with Nicola.

Suddenly, our phones started pinging all over the place. Lucy Victoria was calling Nicola all kinds of names as if she'd took her man. But I'd not been seeing Lucy Victoria for weeks; as far as I knew, it had faded out. We'd not been talking or anything. That's where Nicola's dislike of Lucy Victoria came from; Nicola hadn't taken anyone's man. I'd just decided that I wanted Nicola, not a Playboy model.

Fast-forward 18 months to the Ramabeletsa fight, and I was due to get married to Nicola the next month. The last thing I wanted was for anything at all to get in the way of us getting married.

That's when I got the text message from Nicola telling me that Lucy Victoria was the ring girl. I remember walking to the ring, thinking 'Fuck! Why does this have to happen to me?'. I wasn't even thinking about the fight, I was just thinking about Nicola and Lucy Victoria. The fight started. The bell went for the end of Round 1 and I could hear Nicola shouting abuse at Lucy Victoria as she paraded the round card around the ring. I was thinking 'why does this have to happen to me?'

I don't remember as much as I should about the actual fight, because my head was spinning with everything else. In boxing, you've got to focus on the fight. I do remember the end. In round 5, he wobbled me. I threw a shot back and wobbled him. He caught me with another shot. Glyn threw the towel in. I couldn't understand why, I was sure that I was okay to carry on, but who knows? My head was mashed with everything else. I wasn't thinking about the fight.

When Lucy Victoria was the ring girl for that fight, part of me used to think that Glyn had organised it as a tit-for-tat bit of revenge because he'd been cross with me about something else a few weeks before. Much later, Glyn told me that it hadn't been anything like that at all. That made a certain amount of sense actually. He'd do 'owt to get us back for things, but he wasn't going to mess about with a professional boxing match. My head was mashed, I fought like it, and my comeback ended in disaster.

Back in my amateur days, I'd fought a young lad called Gavin McDonnell and his brother Jamie. I'd been absolutely robbed on the points decision, so when Gavin turned pro I was absolutely convinced that I could take him. Even coming on the back of injuries and two defeats, I thought I could stop him. He was undefeated with 8 wins and a draw out of his nine fights, and on the way up. I liked the idea of being at the top level. All I'd grown up with was being around people that were at the top level. In my contract with Ricky Hatton, who I'd signed up with to promote me before the Craig Lyon fight, I could fight separately if Glyn Rhodes did a promotion. Glyn had a show coming up at the Doncaster Dome, and was in talks with Steffy Bull, Gavin's trainer and manager. Glyn told me that Gavin was on a winning streak. It's a big fight, he told me. It was a Central Area title, with a view to moving on to the English or British title fight next. It was certainly a risk but it provided a clear way forward for my career.

I trained so hard, like it was for a world title, but I believed in my head that it was going to be a walk in the park. I'd badly underestimated Gavin. He's a top lad, someone I've got so much respect for now. We're friends outside the ring, so there was no bad-mouthing each other before the fight. It was all respectful - in fact, we went out together for a Nando's after the fight with Nicola, his missus Sophie, and his boy Carter. The fight itself was one I'd rather forget: he caught me by surprise, landing some really heavy shots in the second round, and knocked me down. That's what happens when you underestimate an opponent. Gavin's moved up to fights at world level since then; he's a proper fighter.

The problem was, it made three losses in a row. Now even the Sheffield Star started to question where my career was going. I started to think about retiring.

It was time for another comeback fight, but - as often happens when things aren't going so well - you fall out with someone. It led to a daft falling out with Glyn Rhodes. He'd got a bill on at the Concord Leisure Centre, where Dave Fidler was fighting for a Central Area title. Glyn booked me on that show as yet another comeback fight, but there was a problem. He phoned me up a day or two before the fight to say that he couldn't get an opponent for me. I was a big hitter, still seen as a threat and a potential title contender. Promoters weren't wanting to take the risk of pitting a hungry young fighter against me, because I might knock out their prize asset. There aren't that many journeymen around at my weight, and I'd already fought most of them and/or they were already fighting that night. For a bigger promoter, that would be no problem: they'd simply pay a journeyman to fly over from somewhere in Central Europe and the job would be complete. Glyn didn't really have the money to do that, but I'd sold tickets for the fight.

He didn't really know what to suggest, and ended up telling me that there was a lad at another gym who was planning on turning pro. Would I be interested in doing an exhibition bout instead? I said 'I'm not doing that, I've sold tickets for this'. Concord was right in my backyard really. It all ended with a 'fuck you then' text from Glyn to me.

I turned up after the show, watching Dave Fidler win the title. He boxed really well. The next morning I texted Glyn, asking him a few questions about what had happened. I didn't want anything like it to happen again, because I'd felt that the whole situation had let my fans down. Glyn just said "I've decided I'm going to get rid of deadwood from the gym. Don't contact me again, don't come back to my gym." Fewky and Carl told me they'd sort it out, but as the weeks went on nothing seemed to be changing. I didn't want to go anywhere else; I'd been with Glyn since I was 10 years old. After 17 years of training with Glyn, I'd got no interest in moving on. Lots of people stay married for less time than that these days. Glyn's always been a bit more than just a great mate. He was like a second dad to me in a lot of ways. I'd travelled the world with Glyn, right back to the days in New York, the Boxing Hall of Fame and Laila Ali when I was a kid.

The thought of another trainer and a new gym filled me with horror. Retirement was suddenly well and truly on the cards, and I started thinking about where I was going to go next in life. My contract with Ricky Hatton Promotions had expired, so I didn't have a trainer, promoter or manager. Apart from that, I'd got a great setup. It really did feel like the end of the road. I felt, though, that I still had a lot to offer - a lot to prove. I really didn't want to retire, and that meant moving on to a new trainer.

I picked up the phone to my mate Curtis Woodhouse, who'd turned from professional footballer to boxer - and who would eventually pick up English and British titles, before going into football management. He was training at Dave Coldwell's gym in Rotherham, but Ryan Rhodes (no relation to Glyn) was training him. Curtis told me that he was trying to persuade Ryan to get his trainer's licence.

In the meantime, I'd phoned around a few places and a few people told me 'I want dead wood'. I spoke to Dennis Hobson Jnr, who used to work with Clinton Woods many years earlier and was interested in giving me a chance by promoting me. He worked closely with Chris Smedley down at Lower Manor Boxing Club. I also spoke to Dave Coldwell. I'd gone from having no options to having a few.

I went down and did a bit of training with both Chris Smedley and Ryan Rhodes. Finding the right trainer is all about finding someone who's on your wavelength and understands how to get the best out of you. There was nothing wrong with Chris Smedley, it's just that something clicked straight away with Ryan. Ryan would never try to completely change my style, just to polish it and refine it. He stood me in front of a mirror, made me go right back to basics and forced me to move in the right way. I'd be going up and down in a straight line and he'd be drilling it all into me, watching my every move - just like Bessey used to do on the Army Boxing Team. I needed that discipline; he didn't just tell me what to do, he made me. As Ryan was just starting out as a trainer, there was usually just me and Curtis in the gym - plus a few others who just came in to work on their fitness. That meant there were people for us to do some body-sparring with (like Ryan Poulter, who was Ryan's dad's business partner), but he'd focus on us. Glyn had more clients, so there was less one-to-one attention. Now, my training seemed more focused.

The choice of Ryan was easily when everything clicked. Even when I was a kid, Ryan Rhodes was one of my heroes along with Herol Bomber Graham, Paul Silky Jones, Clinton Woods and Naseem Hamed. I'd always been a local lad. They were all local boxers; local heroes. Ryan was just starting out back then, but he's very highly rated in the business now. He'd been in with the best when he was boxing, and he knew how to get his knowledge across.

It was soon 2014, and the clock was ticking as I was already 27 years old. I had to start getting on with it if I was going to get anywhere, which ended up meaning three fights in just two months. First off, Dennis matched me up at the Octagon Centre in Sheffield with the Georgian journeyman Levan Garivashbili. He was no pushover, just someone who lost as many fights as he won. The main aim was to come through the fight, put on a performance, get my fan base back fighting on my home turf, and return to winning ways. It was all just about getting me back into the mix. The fight itself was as routine as a comeback can be on the back of three defeats. I stopped him in round 3.

Less than four weeks later, Dennis had a world title fight on in Newcastle. Stuey Hall, who'd fought in his typical valiant style to win the IBF Bantamweight title against Vusi Malinga, now had a tough defence against Martin Ward. I wanted to be on that bill. Dennis was sceptical, telling me that "it's in Newcastle, you won't sell many tickets". I always sold tickets, and promised him that I'd make sure it was worth his while. In the end, at just a couple of weeks' notice, I sold £4,000 worth of tickets. Some of my squaddie mates came down from Edinburgh from the Army base; others travelled up from Sheffield. Newcastle wasn't the worst venue for me in that sense! In my previous fight, I'd been up at super-bantamweight but I promised Dennis that I could still do bantamweight. I slimmed down to the weight, and he found Valentin Marinov as my opponent. I weighed in bang under the 8 stone 6 limit, back down to bantamweight where I felt most comfortable. It was a big event, so the weigh-in was at the Metro Centre round the corner in Gateshead. I was starting to feel ill, I kept coughing and my nose was running. Mark got me a honey and lemonade. Knowing how far everyone had travelled for the fight, I thought there was no way I could let them down.

Thankfully, it was only a 4-round fight. I'd have been able to stop him if I'd been healthy, but I felt shocking. I took the Calpol and a comfortable 40-36 points win. That was the main thing. I'd proved to Dennis that I could sell tickets, too. That impressed him: Dennis was always a keen businessman. Once I'd recovered, Dennis matched me only a few weeks later with Malkhaz Tatrishvili. This was my third fight in just over two months, and I knocked him out in the fifth round of a 6-round contest.

Chapter 18

PAYING THE COST TO BE THE BOSS

The Boss was back in business, and back on a winning streak. Dennis told me to rest for the summer, then prepare for a show at the Octagon in mid-September. I was just two and a half weeks away from that fight, a bit skint, doing a bit of work between training sessions, painting fences for my brother-in-law for a job in town. It was a red-hot day, and it seemed like everyone was walking past and heading to the pub. I thought 'I wish *I* was in the pub'. What harm could it do, after all? My fight was nearly 3 weeks away, so I went across to Dennis' pub down Kelham Island. As often happens when I'm down the pub, I found myself having a few too many. One's too many, and ten's not enough.

I woke up the next day, got straight on the road and went for a run. Then the phone rang. It was Chris Smedley.

"How are you feeling? How's training?"

"Yeah, the fight's still 2½ weeks away but I wish it were this Saturday."

"Do you wanna fight for the Commonwealth title?"

"When?"

"This Saturday…"

Unbeknownst to me, Martin Ward had just pulled out of his Commonwealth title defence against Jason Cunningham due to a chest infection. He was happy to vacate, provided he had a guarantee of being able to challenge to win it back from whichever boxer held the title. Dennis just wanted to win the belt; we could give any guarantee like that if it meant a shot at the Commonwealth.

"Martin Ward pulled out. We need to find an opponent for Cunningham. If we can get the Board to confirm it, it'll be for the Commonwealth title."

I wished that we hadn't had that drinking session. I phoned Ryan and explained the situation.

"Well how do you feel?", he asked. "I think I could do this, Ryan". He looked up Cunningham's record. It was a perfect record: 12-0. They told me that Cunningham had never lost a round in professional boxing, let alone a fight. I looked it up, and I think he might have lost one round in September 2013 against Kyle King.

Ryan got to work, doing his job - watching all the footage. He got me straight down to Dave Coldwell's gym and put me through

10 solid rounds on the pads. He believed in me. I suppose that's a trainer's job, to believe in their fighter no matter what. At the very least, if they don't believe their fighter's going to win, they'd need to be a convincing liar. But I'm sure Ryan believed in me from the start. I'm not sure how many people really believed that I could win the Commonwealth title at such short notice. There were basically just him, Nicola, my mum and dad who seemed convinced.

All hell broke loose. This was a big title, so the media interest in my career suddenly exploded once more. Television - Calendar TV and Look North, radio, newspapers, the phone ringing off the hook from press and from well-wishers. I was preparing for a fight; I was the centre of attention. I absolutely loved it. This is what I'd been dreaming of. When you're in the limelight, your phone never stops ringing.

Behind the scenes, my team were scrambling into action to change the plan. Paul Russell (mind coach) and Stuart How (my NLP coach - neuro-linguistic programming) and Michael Lovett (conditioning coach) who I'd met in Tenerife - were quickly in touch. Cunningham was already the English champion. It moved so fast that I barely had time to think. That might not have been such a bad thing after all. In the midst of all the mayhem I had to sell tickets as quickly as I could. My fans were spread around the country, so it wasn't easy for them to all get there. I wanted to have my supporters there to see the biggest night of my life so far; many of them made it, but others couldn't get there at such short notice.

It was a bit like going into the lions' den. Jason was a local Doncaster lad, so all the locals were rooting for him. I got to the Doncaster Dome, and they'd put me into the same changing rooms as I'd been in for my loss against Gavin. There was a time when I used to be superstitious, but now I believe that you make your own luck. I wanted to ask them to move me to a different changing room, but I thought it through a bit more. This is *my* night, this is *my* time. I'm gonna own it. I'm gonna make this the lucky changing room. The referee came into the changing rooms. It was Ian-John Lewis, who'd stopped me when I took a knee against Haskins. I made a point of reminding him that I could take some hammer, and not to stop the fight if I took the odd punch.

All the crowd seemed to be cheering for Jason Cunningham. The boos for me changed to cheers for him. If it'd been a fight back in the day, they'd have been chucking nobbins into the ring.

But even just at a few days' notice, some of my staunchest fans were there to support me. Fellow boxer Lee Appleyard, who went on to win an English title, and a lad from my 1LI days called Blakey.

Title fights, at British level and above, are fought over 12 rounds. I'd taken a 12-rounder at just a few days' notice. I'd never gone beyond 7 rounds, and that was all the way back in 2009. To win this, it would have to either be a knockout or a marathon. I had heart though. When I was a kid, I always said that I loved the Barrera v Morales trilogy of fights. I'd always wanted to win a big title like they did, a proper war.

What happened next would prove to be more than I'd bargained for. I ended up looking like Avatar after it. Even the ref's shirt was covered with blood by the end; whether it was mine or Jason's, I've no idea. Probably both.

Ross Burkinshaw, with a number of defeats and injuries behind him, a man on a mission in last-chance saloon for making it at world level, determined not to let the opportunity slip. Jason Cunningham, the Iceman, known for remaining cool, calm and collected under pressure, who'd never tasted defeat as a professional. Cunningham was a southpaw, but I was determined not to let that worry me: I'd learned a lot since my Haskins fight.

The fight was close from the first round. Although I'd technically got a slightly longer reach, I was a little crouched down in my style. Perhaps, I thought afterwards, I'd been too crouched down. I was always my own worst critic. At range, he was able to land more shots. Up close, I was landing upper-cuts and hooks. I wasn't going to get through this without taking punches. It's stating the obvious, but the idea is to make him miss or at least take his punches on my gloves - then make sure that my own are landing solidly. In round 1, my shots were more solid than his. We'd get up close, and I'd force him back. The bell rang, sending me back to my stool.

#believeandachieve

Every time I went back to the corner, that's the first thing Ryan would say to me before he'd give me any technical advice. As a boxer, you have to believe in your ability to win the fight. Round 1 was mine; I don't think any neutral could possibly dispute that. We'd traded blows, but the ones I landed were cleaner and more powerful. Cunningham now knew this wasn't going to be a walk in the park against a late-change opponent at short notice. I was determined to melt the Iceman.

Round 2 continued in the same way, following the formula that would determine the rest of the fight. It was all trading punches, and I'd clearly listened to Ryan when he'd drilled into me the importance of head movement. The same clash of styles was evident: at range, he'd land punches. When it was up close, I was winning. Was it an even round? Hard to say. Bystanders at ringside would have scored a lot of the rounds however they personally wanted to see them. It was that kind of fight.

That's not how I used to fight normally. One of the reasons I'd never gone beyond round 7 before is that I tended to either stop my opponents or get stopped. Normally, seeing Ross Burkinshaw on the card meant it'd be an easy night for the judges. Not this night though.

By Round 3, my confidence was growing - it became clear that he couldn't hurt me. The best way to demoralise someone in a fight is to take their best punches and keep on walking forwards. You've taken everything away from them. If he's got nowt else in his locker, I'm destined to win the fight. He'd have to hit me with a sledgehammer to change things. We were both landing punches; he landed more of them, but mine were better quality shots when they landed. It's the age-old question in boxing: quality versus quantity, the stuff that split decisions are made of.

The next few rounds continued according to the same formula. One round started to blur into the next as we went to war, two fighters determined to give no quarter, black eyes and bloody noses never in short supply. I caught him with a great right hook to the jaw; he moved to the body with a few right hands. I felt I was winning the rounds as my punches had more spite; his corner might well have thought they were winning through sheer volume of punches.

Ian John-Lewis knew I could take the pain

Respect. That's one thing that oozes out of you from every pore when you're a genuine boxer. Every press conference I've ever had, I have the utmost respect for anybody. It takes guts to step into that ring, one man against another in brutal, medieval style. It takes guts, especially if you're staring into the eyes of someone like me, Ross The Boss, and my power. My strength and speed versus his reach and boxing.

Round after round, exhaustion creeping onwards, the Championship rounds where heart means more than anything else. The bell rings for the start of the final round, Round 12. Ryan is in the corner, screaming and yelling at me, knowing that all-important point might make the difference in such a close fight. If it wasn't a war before, it certainly was now: defence gave way to attack, both of us determined not to fail to wring a single drop of sweat out of our aching, tiring bodies. Punches which would have fallen harmlessly onto gloves in earlier rounds now hit the target; even holding your hands up to protect your face becomes a supreme task. Arms ache from top to bottom; it's as though you're holding heavy weights in each hand. I trained for that; often, I'd shadow-box literally holding weights to prepare me for this feeling. After 36 minutes of professional boxing, strength is sapped but dogged determination - if anything - grows. I can't imagine going through all that only to watch the belt being handed to my opponent instead. That would be too much to bear. Dennis was standing there in a Ross The Boss t-shirt. His hands towards his face, barely able to watch the action, looking almost as though he was praying for the judges to see it his way.

The crowd wasn't warming just to their chosen fighter, but to the spectacle of bravery and primal instinct. As the final bell approached, even neutrals were on their feet cheering either me, or Jason, or perhaps both of us on. Finally, after the longest 3 minutes of my life, the bell rang. I'd done enough to win…hadn't I? I'd paid the price. By the day after the fight, I looked like the Elephant Man as my face had swollen up so much.

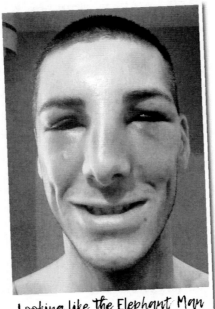

Looking like the Elephant Man

I thought I'd won, but then that's what I thought as an amateur when I'd fought Jamie and Gavin McDonnell.

I'd known my fair share of disappointment from decisions in my time. I always thought I was winning my fights, but this was different. Ryan was celebrating too. Now all eyes were on the judges, in a fight that could reasonably be seen either way. If there's anything longer than three minutes of boxing, it's a minute of waiting between the end of a fight and the result being announced.

"Ladies and Gentlemen", announced the MC, "You have witnessed a contest well worthy of the Commonwealth title. Please show your appreciation once again for both boxers." He didn't need to ask; the applause was already drowning out anything he was actually saying.

"After 12 sensational rounds of boxing, we go to our judges' scorecards. We have a split decision.

Judge Phil Edwards scores the contest 116-112 in favour of Ross Burkinshaw.

Judge John Keane scores the contest 115-113 in favour of Jason Cunningham.

Judge Michael Alexander scores the contest 116-113 in favour of your winner, and new Bantamweight Champion of the Commonwealth…"

For the first time in my career, those words didn't actually tell me the result. Neither of us held the title. Time now seemed to stand still, not helped by the MC's actual pause to build tension and anticipation, as if that were needed.

"…from…Sheffield". That was it, everybody knew. My corner erupted, going absolutely wild at the result. I was lifted up on Ryan's shoulders as the MC tried to announce "Ross Burkinshaw" over the noise of the crowd.

I'd finally made it. I'd been Champion of England, now I was Champion of the Commonwealth.

Nicola was straight into the ring to kiss me after the fight. If anyone knew what I'd been through over the past few years, it was her. It meant so much, having her there to share it with me. They say the three sweetest words in the English language are 'I love you'. I know three more that could give them a run for their money.

And the new....

Chapter 19

MAFIA BOSS?

"People will always talk about you, especially when they envy you and the life you live. Let them. You affected their lives, they didn't affect yours."

As a professional boxer in the Army, I was effectively on the recruiting team. I'd do different events with the Army, and recruitment billboards with my face on them were plastered all over the country. I had an apartment in Sheffield which they paid for - water, gas, electricity and everything. They even covered the TV Licence for me. My apartment was directly above the Vodka Revolution bar in Sheffield.

Living the life I was, it was difficult not to go out partying with my mates all the time. Even more so when I was single, I'd got used to having someone around me all day, every day, 24/7 when I was back at the Army barracks. That transition from having everything planned out for you, to living on your own, takes a lot of adjustment. The Army were absolutely top-notch and looked after me in the most amazing way, and I wouldn't change it for the world. No matter what, though, there's something tough about going from Army life to civilian life. They say that there's a suicide of a serving or former member of the Armed Services every two weeks, and I can believe it. At the barracks, I was used to not even being able to take a shower without someone else being there. Now, everything was so quiet. When I first turned pro, I was really strict about not going out partying with my mates in the run-up to a fight. Later on in my career, that slipped a little bit. Whenever I'm on my own, I just want to seek other people out so that I'm with somebody. I'm sure that comes from my Army days. It got a bit better once I had Nicola and the kids.

I was earning decent money, but living that lifestyle, I was spending at least as fast as I could earn. Boxing expenses were going on the credit card, paid off only after a fight when I'd got the lump sum back in. No more double bubble for me! So, I'd start to work a bit on the side as well as for the Army. My sponsor put me in touch with this short, fat guy called Alan who had the worst wig you've ever seen in your life. He seemed like a nice bloke and he had lots of money, driving a flash car and spending money like he was loaded. It was always first-class travel, steaks, wine, champagne and good hotels when working for him, something else I started to develop a bit of a taste for. I'd get my kit paid for and some of the costs of my training paid too.

He was working in the scrap metal business and wanted to have on-call security protection. If there's one thing I knew, it was how to fight. I could defend myself at all times, I could defend someone else at all times. From the square ring to Army riot training, I knew what I was doing. It sounded much better than working on the doors of local nightclubs, where someone would always take a pop at me because I'm small or because they recognised me and wanted to test their fighting skills.

He'd get me to drive over to wherever he was, and either make sure he was okay, or deliver things for him securely. To protect his money from being stolen, he'd send me to drive a package of money to somewhere. I was doing this for a good 18 months, maybe 2 years in total. It never really occurred to me that there could be anything illegal going on, driving large sums of money from place to place in brown envelopes, largely because I'm a complete idiot. That is, I had no idea at all until the day that I got a phone call from my dad. I was training for a fight with Jason Booth down in Nottingham at the time, though the fight got called off in the end. My dad told me that the CID had been around to the house to arrest me. I handed myself in to the police and got locked up for the day. My phones and laptops were taken, my house was raided. Looking back now, and from what people have told me since, I'm pretty sure I'd been followed by SOCA for over a year to different places, seeing me going here, there and everywhere. Little did I know what I'd been caught up in: there were over 40 people involved in one way or another. The police were apparently investigating fraud and money laundering, something I swear down I knew nothing about. When I was arrested, I was in the Sheffield Star sports section that same day. The police thought they'd found the criminal mastermind behind the plot. "If you don't know everything that's going on", they asked me triumphantly, "how come everyone's got you down in their phone contacts as being the Boss?"

I was, and still am, the Boss - but I'm the boss of 15 foot by 15 foot. Nobody messes with me in there. I'm not the boss of some shadowy criminal organisation, if I was I wouldn't have been stuck with so much debt. I said to the police "You want to know why I'm called the boss in people's phones? Just look at that newspaper. It's right there in black and white." They didn't know what I meant, but I was insistent and showed them. There I was, The Boss all over the newspaper right in front of them. I think they believed me. They were gutted.

I was bailed, and whilst this was all ongoing all kinds of things had happened. I'd got married in Cuba, honeymooned in the Maldives, and took the kids to Egypt for Christmas. As for the Army, I was part of the second tranche of redundancies. The Colonel phoned me and said that I was on the list. The battalion wanted me back soldiering, and I wasn't doing so much recruitment for the Army by this time, so they made me redundant and paid me off. The £23,000 redundancy money (which came in on 12/12/12) bankrolled me for a while, and I did at least put some of that away under the mattress for safekeeping, then spent some on paying off credit cards and taking the family on holiday, but of course the police saw me continuing to spend money like it was water. They weren't wrong, but the money wasn't coming from crime. It was because I was being paid effectively for three jobs and then got a big redundancy package on top. I was spending that much money because I wasn't thinking about the future, not through being high up in some strange criminal plot.

Looking back at it all now, I've got to laugh. It's so funny how people can put 2 and 2 together and make 5, seeing one lifestyle and assuming it's something else. These things are hanging over your head for years; it wasn't until September 2017 that I got the all-clear and they finally dropped the case. There were years of worry, not least because of Nicola and the kids.

Chapter 20

FROM BERET TO BOSS

There's moments in life where something changes, where you just get into the zone and everything clicks into place. Winning the Commonwealth belt did that for me. Suddenly, everyone was interested in Ross the Boss. Many of them didn't know that it takes 20 years to make an overnight success. The next Saturday, I was showing off my Commonwealth belt at Sheffield Wednesday's match away at Bolton.

Showing off my Commonwealth Belt at Bolton v the Owls

I was due to defend the Commonwealth title against Terry Broadbent on February 21st 2015, but Dennis was a man in a hurry - and there were rumours flying around that Terry was going to pull out of the fight. I was a man in a hurry too, ready to keep going forwards. The clock was ticking, and if I was ever going to make it at world level, I needed to step up in the world rankings. The way to do that was to fight for the European title, so Dennis matched me with the tough Belgian opponent Benjamin Smoes.

Ryan kept on at me in the run-up to the fight, pushing me to develop my jab. At world level, you've got to be able to keep them off with a strong jab. I loved to throw all the shots, but your jab's your bread and butter, your go-to weapon in boxing. The Commonwealth fight with Jason Cunningham had been the first time I'd gone the full 12 rounds of boxing, but that was a brutal war. I needed to make sure that I could control fights at this level as well. In theory, the European belt with the WBO was a step up from the Commonwealth title. In practice, I'm not so sure that it was. Smoes hadn't really fought anyone of note. He'd got a 9-3-1 record including a loss by disqualification, which was a reasonable record. But that record was a bit flattering: he'd fought mostly journeymen and didn't have any really good wins on his record. He'd gone 7 rounds with Conlan though, which showed he was no mug, but I was absolutely certain that I could take him. If I wasn't, I'd have had no business stepping in to the ring.

I was supposed to be properly the centre of attention on that night. The whole event - titled "Who's The Boss?" was named after me, just as I like it, but yet again there was a 'will he, won't he?' story. That one was absolutely nothing to do with me. On the undercard, two young up-and-coming young Sheffield boxers - Muheeb Fazeldin and Uzair Najib - were due to face each other.

They'd both sparred together over the years, and both wanted to be the top dog in the Asian community in the city. It was a proper grudge match, a wild swinging encounter with neither fighter thinking anything about defence. Fazeldin won when the referee stepped in to stop it after Najib had been down twice in the first round. The bad blood spilled over, with the closest thing to a riot you'd see at a big match like this. Security were ready to stop a few people trying to force their way down to the changing rooms, but this was a flood of dozens of people. The security guards tried to form a line to protect the steps, then got pushed flying out of the way down the stairs as the angry supporters charged past. Given everything that was going on, there was a real risk that the whole fight could be cancelled. I wasn't worried about beating Smoes, but I was certainly worried about not getting the chance to beat him. Fortunately, everything was calmed down and the evening continued.

When it came to my fight, I have to say that the atmosphere on the night was absolutely unreal. The Octagon centre is a big enough venue to fit thousands, but the seating is really close to the ring and the acoustics make for great crowd noise. We really played that one up, determined to psyche me up and intimidate my opponent before it even got started. I'm pretty sure that Smoes had never seen anything like it. It wasn't just me coming in to the ring with a few of my Army mates, we really went to town on it. We had Coldstream Guards and the Yorkshire Regiment drumming me into the ring in traditional military fashion. In keeping with the military theme, I was wearing khaki shorts for the fight - emblazoned with 'Mrs. B' - Mrs. Boss, or as Dennis Hobson Snr used to call her, the Boss's Boss. I had several sponsors for this fight: people really wanted to be associated with me.

In the Octagon Centre, the changing rooms are downstairs. I went up the stairs, where there's a 'secret' stage entrance at the back. Everyone was shouting, screaming. The soldiers walked forward; the drummers started drumming. That was all the inspiration I needed; the hair standing up on the back of my neck. I remember little snippets, like photographs, from that ring walk. Seeing Nicola, my mum and dad, her friends, my friends, and Dennis Hobson Snr. They drummed me up till I got to the ring - then, silence. The music started to play - Hot Chocolate, You Sexy Thing, taking me back to my Bideford days and stopping that kid in the first round when Sheffield Boxing Centre had taken that trip to Devon. Back to reality, back to the fight. 'This is it', I thought. I reminded myself that Smoes had gone 7 rounds with Jamie Conlan for the European super-flyweight belt, so I knew he was no mug. I'd not watched the footage of him. I never watched 'owt before a fight; that's my trainers' job. I knew I'd got a fight on my hands.

Some of the lads from the Army would always march with me into the ring, often at short notice. At these fights I'd be surrounded by pals like Anthony Blakemore, Gareth Jackson, Robert Blades, John Fleming, Phil Guy, John Chadwick, Mark Skelton and Shane Kay.

In the end, the ring entrance lasted longer than the fight. I came out, quicker to the jab than my opponent, making him miss with the wild punches he was throwing. I'd land a shot, then duck out of the way of his. Just under two minutes into the fight, I could sense something was different when I landed a couple of shots. He seemed to be wobbled by my power, but I hadn't properly got going yet. He threw another wild punch. I slipped it, then put in a thumping right hook to the body. He went straight down. He beat the count, still looking unsteady on his legs. I knew there wasn't long left in the round. I didn't want to give him a minute's rest and the chance to recover. When you've got a chance to finish a fight, you finish it. Strange things can happen when you don't take your chances in boxing. So straight away, I was on him - and knocked him down with a left to the face. The ref didn't even count, stopping the contest instantly.

…And the New!

I never tired of hearing those words. This time, they'd catapult me to a no.8 ranking with the WBO and put me firmly on the path to a world title eliminator. Smoes never fought again.

Chapter 21

THE LAST POST

"You gotta know when to hold 'em, know when to fold 'em, know when to walk away, know when to run" - *Kenny Rogers, The Gambler (one of my favourite songs)*

Soldier on. Those two little words describe my attitude to everything in life. How quickly things can change. Three minutes in the ring seems like a lifetime outside; no-one will ever know that until they've stood in my shoes, fought the wars I've fought. The life-changing events happened so suddenly, without any warning. The elbow injury against Mboyane when I'd been on top of the world, taking me from the wave of the high that I'd been on from winning the Commonwealth title, winning the European title, and going down the inter-continental route. When I started picking up those belts it didn't feel like it was just another fight here and there. It felt like destiny, like I was finally making the most of my talent.

Soldier on. That injury against Mboyane wasn't going to stop me either. Time to pick myself up, get my elbow right, and get back in the ring. Lose the battle? Maybe. I was so determined to win the war. Heartache, heartbreak, determination that I had to find a way to come back and do the thing that I'd loved doing more than anything: underneath the lights and the television cameras, one man against another, the ultimate test of strength and resolve.

Soldier on. Gavin McDonnell was on his own world-title journey. He needed proper quality sparring opponents, I needed money. When a boxer's between fights, what are they supposed to live on? Dave Coldwell's camp offered to pay me well enough: £50 per round for a spar. It's not like I didn't need to get some rounds in the bank myself as part of my comeback. I could give Gavin as good as I got, so doing half a dozen rounds with him would get some cash in my pocket and keep us both sharp at the same time. It was a no-brainer for me. My mates would say that I'd fight for free, you don't need to pay me. They had a point. The first round of sparring was going fine. In the second, I must have over-reached slightly when throwing a right hand to the body. My shoulder erupted in the same pain. I had to go straight to hospital.

Soldier on. The pain, the operation, more titanium screws, more pain, panic about the future, about my career, my credit cards and debts nobody knew about, what I was going to do next, my life and career exploding around me just as my shoulder was exploding in pain. All I'd known was being a boxer. What next?

Soldier on…

Chapter 22

ROCKY ROAD

"Holding on to anger is like grasping a hot coal with the intent of throwing it at someone else. You are the one getting burned."

I don't think anyone can really understand what I was going through when I had to retire, unless they've been there themselves. My whole life, since I was 8 years old, revolved around boxing. I've always been a fighter, always a boxer, always ambitious to be the best at whatever I do. I was ranked no.8 in the world with the WBO, no.11 with the IBF, and rising fast when suddenly that shoulder injury exploded and forced me to retire.

I'd had a dislocated shoulder back in 2008, and I'd come back from it. I'd had a dislocated shoulder in 2011, and had to have a titanium screw put in. In 2012, I had cruciate ligament surgery on my left knee. This time, though, it was worse. It was more than just a shoulder dislocation - this needed a bone graft (and more pins) to repair a fractured shoulder socket. It's such a frustrating injury, because there are times when I can punch without a problem. With a lot of luck, I could probably have fought again - but there are some shots that I just daren't risk throwing. The thrill of a comeback would be amazing, but I couldn't do justice to myself if I did. I don't want to be the latest in a long line of boxers fighting on beyond the point where the body won't let me. There were times, though, when I was really tempted to try.

What next? What was left in life for me? It's easy to roll with the punches when you're winning, but what happens when it feels like your life's passion has been taken from you? I'd even met my wife, Nicola, through boxing. When I'd been out injured once before, I'd spent the time running training sessions - and Nicola walked into the gym. So when I was suddenly no longer the champion boxer, all kinds of worries went through my mind. I wouldn't be human if they didn't.

In fact, Nicola was absolutely amazing back then. She stuck with me through thick and thin. It's like all that stuff in the wedding vows: for richer for poorer, in sickness and in health.

You can you tell a lot about your mates, too. I know which of my mates were there for me not just when I was winning, but when I was losing, or in hospital or when I'd done my shoulder in too. The most incredible people in life are those who are there to help you even when it's a one-way street for a time, when you've hit rock bottom and you've got nothing to give back. I was just thinking about how lucky I am to have loads of mates like that, and I got a call from my mate Grant Horsfield right then. He's one of those guys. A mate I've known from school, not someone I'd write about scrapes with.

Living as a boxer is living on a credit card. You build up expenses throughout the training camp, which are then paid off when you fight. The credit card mounts up, then it's paid. If you're a Tony Bellew, Amir Khan or Kell Brook, an absolute household name who can sell out a stadium for every fight, you have the luxury of being able to live comfortably between fights. For those on the way up, one injury can be brutal financially as well as physically and emotionally. No fight means no credit card payments, and that means spiralling debt and high APRs. I had to laugh a year or so ago when someone suddenly tried to charge me a huge amount of money for a job after I thought I'd negotiated him down. Apparently he'd googled 'Ross Burkinshaw net worth' and an astronomical figure - $700,000 - came up. I actually didn't have a penny to my name, struggling to make even the minimum payment on cards. One day, I couldn't even afford a cup of coffee when meeting a friend in Costa.

Many non-boxing fans don't know that a journeyman boxer can often be better paid than his up-and-coming opponent. New young boxers coming through the ranks haven't yet developed a huge following, or the ability to sell out a fight. Unless they're a big prospect who's going to be on Sky TV, don't expect the promoters to pay out large sums of money. The journeyman, on the other hand, is being paid to get punched. The old 'have gloves, will travel' cliché is so important. They have no real prospect of advancement. They fight week in, week out, at venues small and large up and down the country.

If they're knocked out, they have a mandatory 28-day period without fighting - so they try hard to stay on their feet, learning to avoid heavy punches and give young fighters the elusive 'rounds in the bank' they need to develop experience. In a very different kind of way, you've got to admire people like Kristian Laight, the journeyman who'll probably have managed 300 professional fights by the time this book is published. At the time of writing, he's got 277 defeats - but incredibly, only 5 of those came by way of knockout. There's a skill to what he does, and boxing needs guys like him, but personally I preferred to be the one doing the knocking-out.

If I'd tried to carry on boxing after those injuries, I wouldn't have been the same. I would have, in the end, become basically a high-class journeyman. I could probably have one it, but I'd have to have been really careful with my shoulder. There are just some shots that, even now when I'm demonstrating them to clients in my gym, I don't feel confident enough to throw. There's a reasonable amount of money in being a good journeyman. I mean being the kind of person who can give a fight to a young prospect who's going up to world level. Think about it this way. When a young Anthony Joshua was knocking everyone out in his early career, he couldn't find anyone to stand up to him. In his first ten fights, I think he only actually completed 8 full rounds of boxing - he knocked that many people out in the first round without ever finishing a round. Eddie Hearn put him in with Kevin Johnson, who'd gone 12 rounds with Vitali Klitschko and Tyson Fury and never been stopped. He was supposed to take Joshua the distance. He only made it to the second round. At that time, can you imagine how much Eddie Hearn would have paid to find a fighter who could just stand up to him for 6 or 8 rounds?

A lot of people knock a fighter like Tyson Fury, who didn't really knock so many opponents out on his way up. Fury had bags of talent, and he got himself much more experience by learning his craft and getting the rounds in. He's got power, talk to anyone who's sparred with him, and they'll say that. David Allen always says that you don't feel the power until he really sits down on his punches. Fury probably could have got the knockouts if he'd wanted, but instead he tried different things and developed.

One fight, Tyson Fury surprised everyone by coming out in a southpaw stance. He won the fight, but he'd also gained a skill by doing it. People outside boxing don't always appreciate Fury's technical ability and hand-speed, because they see a lot of his fooling around and talk outside the ring.

When you've got a hungry, young, world-class fighter coming through, there's a fair bit of money in it if you're a high end journeyman able to take a beating for a fair few rounds without getting knocked out. Young fighters need to develop that experience. I had offers for that kind of thing, to take a fight I wasn't physically capable of actually winning because of my injuries. Some promoters knew that I was running short of cash and let's face it, everyone knew that part of me was longing for a comeback. There were three big reasons I didn't do it in the end.

One, what if I'd made my injuries worse? If I put myself out of action and out of work for even longer, for one payday - or if I did the injury in training or sparring so that I didn't even get that payday.

Two, I had to think of Nicola. I don't think she'd have really wanted me to go into a fight under those circumstances. She'd looked after me often enough over the years, the last thing I would have wanted is to put her under even more strain.

Three, and most importantly, it'd betray everything I believe in. I don't go into a fight thinking I could lose. I go into a fight knowing I'm going to win. Without that 100% confidence, going into a fight like that, probably losing to someone a fit Boss would've beaten, I'd not be true to myself or to my fans. The media's not kind to boxers who keep going for too long either. My pride wouldn't ever let anyone call me a washed-up has-been.

So there I was, injured and penniless, desperate for something to come along. At times like that, sometimes you lose a sense of perspective. I found myself asking silly questions about my relationship with Nicola. With professional boxing having been taken away from me, I started to worry about Nicola too. I never really thought she was like that, though. I thought our relationship was based on love, not based on how many belts I can put around my waist. However difficult things might have become since then, she did stand by me through the worst of times, and for that I'll always be grateful.

For months, I couldn't even face watching boxing on television. It was just too painful, thinking that I should be there. I even briefly announced on social media that I was going to make that comeback, however unlikely and difficult that would be. At the time, though, I was just starting to build my future. In the end, after chatting to Nicola and other friends about it, the risks were just too great. Another injury would have been devastating, so reluctantly I had to call it off.

My struggles with depression are well known; I've always been open about it. Why shouldn't I be? I'm not going to pretend that everything's going great when it isn't. I don't want other people who are suffering with the same thing to think that they're on their own, that they're the only person who's ever felt that way. I've always been a bit of a worrier. I overthink everything, but at the end of the day you know that with me what you see is exactly what you get. I've even got the tattoo to prove it: I've got "Life isn't about waiting for the storm to pass, it's learning to dance in the rain" and "Change your thoughts and you change your world" inked on me forever. I'm not going to let myself forget that I'm going to win my fight with depression, that's a struggle that's always with me, but I'm never going to lose to that one.

Posing at my gym #youresorain

Life's a bit like boxing: sometimes you'll be in a long, gruelling fight - and things aren't going your way. You've got to weather the storm, tuck up tight with your defences, bite down hard on your gumshield and suck it up. Sure, you're going to take a few punches - but you're going to protect yourself at all times, so that you're still standing and when you get your opportunity you'll be ready to take it. Dealing with times like this is a bit like my fight for the Commonwealth title with Jason Cunningham: I had to take a lot of punches that night, but I gave as good as I got, came out fighting, and I edged a narrow decision in one of the best fights of the year.

Anyone can suffer from depression, and anyone can have a 'bad round' taking too many shots. If you're in that situation, treat it like a boxing match.

Don't, whatever you do, throw in the towel. We're not quitters. Winners don't quit, quitters don't win - as my old trainer, Glyn Rhodes used to tell me. Make sure you've got good friends in your corner, people you can trust. You can tell your cornerman anything. If you've picked up an injury in the ring, there's no point hiding it from your corner. They need to know, so they can change their instructions to you.

If your depression's serious enough that you need to see a doctor, go see a doctor. I'd never go into a fight without my cut-man. Most of all, when that bell rings, know that you are going to come out fighting - because in this team, we don't back down. Nobody ever won a championship belt by retiring on their stool. Even if you feel like you're behind on the judges' scorecards, you've still got a puncher's chance.

There's people like Daniel 'Miracle Man' Jacobs, who beat cancer, came back, and won a world title. However bad things seem, they're only going to get better. It didn't always feel like that after

I had to retire. It felt like the light at the end of the tunnel was likely to be an oncoming train.

It wasn't easy, either, to come back emotionally after retiring. There were plenty of bumps along the road, even after I'd dusted myself off and got myself back on with the business of living. One thing I do know: if I call myself The Boss, I'm not going to let depression be the boss of me.

Chapter 23

I GET KNOCKED DOWN, BUT BOSS GETS UP AGAIN

Boxing is one of life's great equalisers. I've had a police officer walk out of my gym after training, whilst a drug dealer walks in. Rich people, poor people, men and women, children of all ages, people with varying disabilities, people of all shapes and sizes, some in the peak of physical fitness - and some, well, let's just say a little less fit.

It was a few months after my final fight that I had to announce my retirement. I had a few options in the boxing world. Outside it, I'd have ended up doing a manual job. I don't mind getting my hands dirty and doing a solid day's graft, but boxing's always been my passion. I've had a number of professional fighters ask me to train them, but it wasn't for me. When I was a professional boxer, I didn't need anyone to motivate me. I gave 110% because I wanted to, not because some trainer had to tell me to. I learned from my Army days to turn up on time, or early, to obey instructions, and to give my absolute best all the time. Those things all just came naturally to me anyway. I hold myself to incredibly high standards, and I wouldn't deal well with training any professional boxer who didn't treat it in exactly the same way.

Opening my own gym, well, that's a totally different story. I'm not training professional fighters. I'm training ordinary people who want to develop their fitness. I'm not going to have unrealistic expectations of the people who walk into my gym. They're not professional boxers - their biggest opponents are often themselves. Whether they're looking to develop fitness, learn self-defence skills, lose weight, or even just develop a bit of self-confidence, I can help with all of that. Most of them never step into the ring to do an actual fight. If they do, it's a white-collar event to raise money for charity, and that's a completely different matter.

So when my promoter Dennis Hobson offered me premises to set up my own gym, I took up his offer without too much hesitation. I'd always been close to Dennis. He'd even had us over for Christmas dinner one year. Things aren't quite so great between me and him now, but I'm not going to use my book to have a pop at him. He provided the place, and I started to build my business. Things were okay, and it was nice to have a place where I could train people, but I wasn't really making much money out of it. It takes time to build a business, so perhaps I could eventually have made something out of that gym. I certainly wasn't planning to quit. When it wasn't making much money for me, though, it wasn't making much for Dennis either. In the end, we parted company and I had to find somewhere new.

I moved from there to Grant 'Miffa' Smith's gym in Darnall, where I continued to work at building my business. There, in Darnall, I was surrounded by other gyms and had to make sure

Working the ropes

that I did my training at times which wouldn't inconvenience the amateur and professional boxers that he was training. It was great for Grant to let me work out of there, but the longer I stayed, the more I realised that I needed to have my own place. Makes sense really, when you think about it. If I'm the Boss, I need to be in charge of somewhere - not looking after someone else's place.

It's the old problem though - to get your own place, you need money. To get money, you need your own place. Already stuck with large amounts of credit card debt from the end of my professional boxing days, I didn't really have much capital behind me.

I started looking around at different places. One of them looked like it had last been used as some sort of teen drug den. It needed so much work to get it into any kind of fit state, stuck out of the way on an industrial estate in the middle of nowhere. To succeed in any kind of business, you need to get your location right - and that's where I finally got a break. The Handsworth area of Sheffield didn't really have anything in the way of a boxing gym, and loads of people from the local area would be interested in something like that. An old friend, Jameel Ali, heard that I was looking for a place and allowed me to use part of his premises to set up my own gym. When I set up in there, the loyal clients who'd followed me from Dennis' gym to Grant's gym also followed me to my own gym in Handsworth. It gave me another chance, though, to build something in the local area as well. There were even some times over the summer that I'd trained people in my back garden. Strangely enough, the neighbours didn't really seem to mind very much.

Even the little things were a struggle. It's not just about decorating, buying bags and pads and dozens of pairs of gloves, getting my own boxing ring, signage, and everything else. It's simple things that matter - imagine trying to cover a 1,000 square foot area with specialist flooring for training. The costs really did add up, but the help I got from friends and family just blew me away.

My dad was just amazing, helping with the practical side of things. After a hard week of work, he'd be straight along to the gym to do all kinds of work for me: building changing rooms, the desk, just about any odd job you could imagine. Day in, day out, he'd be down there making a difference.

One of the people who helped me out financially when I moved gyms was Jonathan Arnott. He came to me at 17 stone, never been to a gym before in his life, looking to develop his fitness. He was an independent member of the European Parliament, a very good chessplayer, overweight and unfit. I trained him, believe it or not, for a 'chessboxing' bout which involved playing speed chess and punching each other in the face alternately. When he was put up against a 6 foot 3 bodybuilder with more boxing experience, unsurprisingly he got knocked out. But over time, he developed his skills and lost over 4 and a half stone in weight. Strangely, I never fought at the York Hall - but he did, the first time he boxed.

Jonathan tends to be good at anything I'm bad at: sometimes, when he's training in the gym, I'll ask him a sum like 28 x 32 or something like that. He'll come back with 896 within a couple of seconds. Good practice for chessboxing, I suppose. Jonathan's one of the least practical people you'll ever meet, but he did help me and my dad to assemble the boxing ring in my gym. He also bought the huge canvas prints showing all the combinations I teach my clients, so they're always up on the wall for everyone to see.

"If in doubt, jab it out"

I know I go on a bit about how boxing's like a family, how the Army was like a family, and all that stuff. It's people like Ray Gillott that make me say it. He's over 70 years old now, but he still trains people from time to time down at the gym - and when I set up, he did a lot of work doing some gardening and making the outside look a bit better.

Then there's the odd things that you wouldn't think about. Take scaffolding for example. You'd probably not think about needing that, but when you're putting up 20 or so heavy bags which you'll have 18-stone men punching with force all at the same time, you're going to need some pretty strong framework to hold it all together. Two friends of mine, Craig O'Brien and Dean Lindley, run 7 Hills Scaffolding in Sheffield (like Rome, Sheffield's built on seven hills), and even though we weren't that close by that time, I got it put in for free.

Companies like Rope Access Trade Solutions (you probably *would* expect a boxing trainer to need ropes), Concept Interiors (run by a friend of mine from back at school) and Eden Memorials (through Trevor Parker, who used to train with me and Ryan back at Dave Coldwell's gym) all helped with sponsorship in one way or another. Worksop Timber supplied all the wood I needed. They were great, sponsoring me all through my boxing career too.

A boxer gets paid for what they do as a professional, but they also need sponsorship because there are so many other costs associated with a training camp. Another company, AB Graphics, was a contact from Grant's gym. I'd put something on Facebook

Live about getting my own place, and they got in touch with me. Out of the blue, they offered to do my signage.

I've got all their posters up on the wall of the gym to say thanks. These companies have been so good to me. A lot of it comes from social media, especially Facebook. I'm always having to remove a few friends from my Facebook page because there's a 5,000-friend limit. When I'm meeting new people, I can't add them. That's a lot of people, just such an easy network for finding people and sharing skills. I do them a favour, they do me a favour. Some people want something in return, some just want to help out.

Whether it was painting or decorating, people chipped in. I'd love to mention everyone who helped, it's so many that it'd end up being a list not a book, but special thanks to Martin West, Darren Staniforth, ex-professional boxer Karl Bell, Anthony Turner and his missus, Leanne. Karl Bell only lost once in his short professional career (6-1, no draws), and he was never stopped. He came back to do an exhibition match on my last white-collar show, and you can still see just how polished his skills are.

I keep mentioning names, and there's so many more I could mention. I'm not just building a gym, I'm building a community. Making a success of the gym is proper hard work. Every class, group session, one-to-one, is great fun to do - but I'm often working 13 or 14 hours in the day, and I'll even do some sessions on Saturdays and Sundays. If I didn't take the same 110% attitude that I took towards boxing, I'd be out of business by now. I knew I could make a success of it, and I'm proving that now.

Chapter 24

A HUNDRED NEW STORIES

The story of my professional boxing career may have come to an end, but today I'm just as motivated as I was two decades ago when I stepped into a competitive boxing ring for the first time. Now, it's a new story - not just mine, but hundreds of stories of people I'm training and working with on a daily basis.

I'm writing this chapter just a few days after my biggest charity boxing show yet. We raised thousands for Hallam FM Cash For Kids through sponsorship and then on the day, but to me the event showcased the difference that I've been able to make through my new gym. I'm going to spend some time explaining about just a few of those stories, showing a flavour of what I'm trying to build. It's a work in progress, but I'm so proud of each and every one of those men, women, boys and girls who come into my gym and work hard to achieve something.

One roasting day in July, one of the hottest of the year, we put up a marquee in the car park of my local pub, the Winter Green in Waverley. Emma Thomson, the landlady of the pub, had been training at my gym for a while. She offered to use her premises for the event, which we'd previously held at the New York Stadium in Rotherham. This time though, the atmosphere, holding it in the premises of one of the local pubs, was mega. I get more people come to my white-collar shows than you'd see at most amateur

night cheering for people they didn't even know. It's weird that I now get more comments back when I put on a white collar event than I did when I won my European title! I used to be well known in the boxing world, but now I can't walk round Meadowhall without people coming up and talking to me about the gym. One lady, who'd been at Magna the night I announced my retirement, told me later that my show "was really exciting - better than watching a [pro] boxing fight".

The kids

I started boxing when I was 8, but some of the kids who come down to my gym are even younger than that. The youngest who did it on the day was 4 years old, but I take kids from the age of 3. There's no way that I'm going to have the younger ones fighting, but that doesn't mean they can't get into the ring and showcase their skills. We'd set up a boxing ring in the marquee, and the kids I've been training had the chance to show all the punches, moves and combinations they'd been learning. Just doing something as simple as this gave them the chance to prove what they were capable of - and in front of a large audience, too.

Miley on the pads

The skill level really surprised a lot of the people watching. When you see a 6-year-old delivering crisp combinations, learned perfectly, it's not always what you're expecting. One thing that's really come along in recent years is girls' interest in boxing. People like Nicola Adams and Katie Taylor are proving to be real role models. Down at the pub, it's the landlady who put on a pair of gloves. I know I'm a bit of a hypocrite though, 'cos I don't think I'd cope well if my partner were to ever do a fight!

Shaun and Billy

Shaun Barker suffers from severe cerebral palsy. He needed a stick to walk, but he's a huge boxing fan, and admires Kell Brook more than anyone. His support worker told him about my gym, and I started to do a bit of work training him. When he's in my gym, he's been able to push himself - his passion is boxing, so having the chance to do some work on the pads made all the difference. He's now walking around my gym without his stick. Just that one fact alone would be enough reward for all the hard work, but Shaun's dream was to get into the ring.

Ross and Shaun

One of my friends, Billy 'The Hitman' Greenwood, who actually knows his way around a boxing ring pretty well, agreed to step in with Shaun and allow him to fulfil his dream.

Now, I'm not going to say that the fight was in any way stage-managed. Nobody ever admits anything like that in boxing! Amazingly, just as it seemed that Shaun was tiring a little on a baking-hot summer's day, Billy Greenwood fell to the canvas and couldn't possibly get back up. The crowd erupted, and Shaun got a memory that he'll remember for the rest of his life. "I don't think you realise", one of his support workers said to me afterwards, "just how much you've changed his life." Someone in the crowd said to me "I hadn't cried for 10 years since my grandad died until that happened with Shaun". I'm more of an emotional kind of guy than that: I cried when Hayley died in Coronation Street.

Shaun took his seat, watching the remainder of the boxing bill. I'm so proud of him for how far he's come. I'm so proud of Billy for helping him out. Amazingly, having been 'knocked clean out' just minutes before, Billy made a miraculous recovery to act as cornerman for the blue corner for the rest of the event. In the red corner was Martin Tonk, a great thinking guy, a real strategist with a knack for putting fighters at ease.

Louis and Jonathan

Louis came into my gym as one of the more unlikely characters to step into a boxing ring. Perhaps he was inspired by the landlady of the pub, because he works as the pub's chef. The first day he came in, he looked like he had absolutely no clue. He gave it an amazing go, so that in the couple of months of training, he'd developed his style a little bit more. I was taken aback by how quickly he'd progressed in such a short period of time. Although he didn't manage to win, you could see the development.

Jonathan was, to put it mildly, a little nervous about getting back into the ring after his chessboxing experience. He never stopped training, but the thought of fighting again certainly took its toll on him psychologically. When he got into the boxing ring, he did exactly as he was told - staying behind his jab, controlling the fight, then pressed home the advantage with a flurry of punches I'd never seen from him before, and he was able to win by stoppage just before the end of the first round.

That was on the Saturday. Louis was straight back in the gym, first thing Monday morning. That's what I call commitment.

Mark and James

Weighing over 18 stone, Mark is one of the more imposing figures at my gym. He's taken part in a few white-collar fights before, and he boxed on my first ever white-collar show, but this one was something different entirely. He'd always step in at short notice to help out with anything - whether that's fighting at the last minute, or working as a cornerman.

James, who's used to weights training rather than boxing, decided to give it a go. Watching James in training, he didn't really throw that many punches - which had me a little concerned before their fight. What followed was a 3-round war, lots of body shots being traded without a moment's let-up. Mark was being cautious, avoiding punches to the head because he knows that James suffers from epilepsy. Amazing to think that they were able to put on such a show - we're not talking professional boxers here! Mark was (just) given the decision, but it was an incredible performance from both of them.

Non-boxers often think that boxing is particularly violent and dangerous. They're not wrong about it being violent, that's the nature of it. But with headguards and 16-ounce gloves, what we do is incredibly safe. We do, of course, have paramedics on standby - but you're far more likely to get seriously injured if you're a football player than if you do a white-collar boxing event. This fight did result in an injury: Mark broke a bone in his hand. Hand injuries are probably the most common injury in these circumstances.

Dan and Byrne

As soon as I'd moved into my new place and opened the gym, Dan started coming along to do the boxercise (or Bossercise, as we call it - there is literally nothing that I won't put my name or branding on, if I can find a way of making it work) classes. Like many people, he'd never done anything like this before. He's just a good, honest, hard-working lad - I don't have to write an amazing story about everyone, you can just rely on him to turn up, knuckle down and train hard.

When I say that I'd put my name, picture, and branding on anything, I really mean it. I'm a bit of a Del Boy like that. When I was a kid, I'd sell owt I could get my hands on - always used to say "I could even sell snow t'Eskimos". I've set up 'BossBoxFood' to sell nutritional meals. They're good quality, nothing Del Boy about them! After this event, people were saying that they were seeing so much about it on FaceBook that they barely knew what their friends and family were up to. I joked that it should be renamed 'BossBook'. At least, I think I was joking. Probably.

Dan's opponent pulled out at short notice, leaving me with what I expected to be a huge headache trying to find a replacement opponent. As it happened, that wasn't going to be a problem. Byrne heard that I was a fighter short, and immediately volunteered. Nothing unusual about that, you might think, but Byrne was only 15 years old at the time. For a moment I did wonder about putting a 15 year old in with a grown man, but I've always been a believer in 'if you're good enough, you're old enough'. When I was 15, I would have done exactly the same thing - and I didn't want to deny him the opportunity. He didn't disappoint, with a very high work-rate in the ring. It was hard-fought all the way through.

It wasn't easy for Dan, in a way. The crowd were all on Byrne's side, and there was no real upside to Dan from beating a 15-year-old. He landed a couple of good shots to the face, and the ref - wanting to be very careful - stopped it because Byrne had picked up a nosebleed. If that had happened in a professional fight, you wouldn't dream of stopping it. You've just got to be a bit more careful when it's white-collar.

Scott and Darren

Like Dan, Scott used to turn up to my Bossercise classes. He'd done a white-collar fight once before, but he'd trained with someone else - as far as I know, someone who was a martial arts trainer rather than a specialist boxing trainer. So when he trained with me, we noticed a massive improvement in his skills very quickly. Scott's the kind of person who I can phone up and he'll come down and spar with anyone.

He had a bit of a laugh with his ring-name, and it took a while before everyone cottoned on. Scott 'Awesome' Wells. If you see it written down, you don't think straight away of Orson Welles. He was fighting Darren, who's just a very quiet lad, who wanted to come down and give boxing a go. Each person who comes down has their own reason for doing it, and some you know a bit more about than others. Matched them up because I thought they'd be bang on, but Scott really outperformed expectations. Because Scott had done it before, he was able to deal very well with any nerves. Nerves are a funny thing in boxing. You need to be nervous to perform well, but if you're too nervous it can make you freeze. Scott seemed to be in the zone.

Emma and Kirsty

There's many local pubs where the landlady might need to be a bit tough, but there can't be many where she's stepped into a boxing ring in her own pub grounds to prove she's capable of doing it. Emma spent most of the week doing her job, running the pub, talking to management, meeting sales targets - and being involved in the preparation of the event. You'd expect her to be exhausted enough just from that, let alone having to step into the ring to fight. Rumour has it that when it was her turn to fight, the bar closed for ten minutes: none of her staff wanted to miss watching her! Though to be fair, nobody would want to be at the bar at that moment - they were all far too busy watching her. Emma's opponent also pulled out at short notice. It's showbiz, the show must go on! Kirsty was James' partner, so that was easily sorted as she kindly volunteered to step in.

That was the last thing that could be described as 'kind' about it. Kirsty was more experienced, and that experience did show. Emma punched hard, accurately, and seemed to land some very powerful shots. Kirsty was able to manoeuvre Emma into the corner and deliver a flurry of punches on a few occasions. The sheer volume of punches had the whole audience on the edge of their seats. Emma had shown so much ability, guts and determination. The only thing she lacked was experience.

One thing about boxing, though: we don't judge things on emotion. It's not fair to the fighters to do that. There was a lot of corruption about in my grandad's generation - that's where the old quote comes from: "In Italy, you've got to knock them out to get a draw". We've got to have enough self-respect not to do that. Sometimes, you do get a duff decision in boxing. Different judges can see fights in different ways.

There was to be no 'home' decision this time. Kirsty was declared the winner. This isn't Italy, after all. The fight did, though, win the 'fight of the night' trophy.

Andy and Matt

Matt Bell (not related to Karl Bell) is one of the great, down-to-earth guys at the gym. He loves fighting, and he loves helping out. Andy's a big guy, but it was his first time boxing. One of the difficult things about running an event like this is trying to put together fair matches, but also matches that will be entertaining and the crowd will want to watch. Match-making is easy enough to mess up even when you're dealing with experienced, professional fighters and you've got hours of video footage of them. It's not like I've got an unlimited supply of potential opponents either, I've got to just do the best I can in matching people at the gym.

I try to mix different advantages, play them off one against the other. Taller guys against faster guys, fitness versus power, or in this case Matt's experience against Andy's size. I'm never going to get all eleven bouts absolutely spot on, but I think they were mostly entertaining.

Karl and Timmy

This bout was the 'exhibition' match of the evening: Karl Bell is an ex-professional boxer who only lost once. Timmy is an ex-amateur who fought for a long time at a very high level, including at the ABA finals after sparring at Brendan's gym before turning pro for a couple of fights with Frank Warren. Non-boxing fans might instinctively expect that 'professional beats amateur', but it's not really that straightforward. An experienced amateur might have had a lot more fights than a professional fighter.

One of the most embarrassing events of the evening happened before that fight: it's traditional in boxing to ring the bell, in silence, to mark the passing of a great figure in boxing. Because Timmy had trained with Brendan, it seemed like the appropriate time to do it. I rang the bell ten times to remember the life of the late, great Brendan Ingle. Unfortunately, the bell chose that moment to fall apart and the end fell out. We had to put the bell back together and continue to ring it, but everyone was still very respectful. We said after that Brendan was no doubt watching, somewhere up there, and 'probably did it as a joke to let me know he wa' there'.

Ten bells for Brendan

The fight itself was a beautifully-matched clash of styles, with disagreements in the crowd about who won. We gave it as a draw, which the fighters seemed to agree was a fair result.

Matt and Aaron

Matt Taylor's been with me for a while. He's followed me from Gleadless to Darnall to Handsworth. He's a bus driver, but he still turns up to training on time. After training for a couple of years, he thought he was ready to have a go. Matt's very short, but durable and very fit.

Aaron is completely the opposite. He's a lot bigger in terms of size, but hadn't done very much sparring and had been struggling a bit for fitness. Credit to him, he didn't drop out when a family member got very ill. He'd even brought his wedding forward and got married the week before to make sure that they wouldn't miss the wedding. I thought it'd be a great fight between Matt and Aaron, because of the clash of styles. Aaron's performance was stunningly good for his experience level and interrupted training. On every boxing bill, someone's going to take you by surprise. This time, it was Aaron. Seems he was a man on a mission.

Reece and Ben

Ben's been doing one-to-one sessions with me for a while. He works for another company (LSA meats) that used to sponsor me when I was a professional. His opponent, Reece, is a lovely lad who came to me just a few months ago. Don't get me wrong, I could tell he knew a bit about boxing. I couldn't believe though how much he came on during the three-month training period. Proper quality stuff. The fight was a clash of styles between Reece's reach and Ben's speed. Reece clearly won the fight, but something went wrong. Alan got the fighters confused and - to stunned disbelief from the crowd - announced that Ben had won. So much for 'it'll be alright on the night'. He shrugged his shoulders, announced the correct decision, and said "Oh well, you're not paying me to do this."

Yeah, if I paid someone they'd have done the job right. Seriously, though, Alan was an absolute star. The DJ didn't turn up, so he ended up doing lots of different things at once. He extended the breaks between rounds slightly, because it was such a hot day.

The crowd loved it. If you didn't know they were white-collar fighters, you'd have been sure that fight was at a much higher level. They honestly looked like good quality amateur fighters. You know what? I enjoy that sense of achievement just as much as I would if I were training amateur or professional boxers.

Ricky and Damian

Ricky's the biggest character in my gym. If there's anyone I have to take the mick out of during a session, it's usually him. He doesn't half go at it in sparring, no matter how many times I say 'light'. If I said Ricky's an ex-professional boxer, I wouldn't be lying. He lasted about two minutes though. Aged 27, he walked into a professional gym and said 'I want to be a professional boxer'. He worked hard, trained, got his pro licence (an achievement in itself) and eventually got into his first fight, against a journeyman boxer who'd lost the vast majority of his fights. Ricky froze, took a shot which rearranged the cartilage in his nose, and the fight was stopped. He's a fighter though; he doesn't mind fighting anyone.

He wrote a book, Cinderella Boxing, which featured me and a number of other professional boxers who'd had different struggles outside the ring. His favourite chapters were about the journeymen, because they're remarkable stories that nobody ever really tells. He's passionate about his book and about helping with homelessness.

His opponent was Damian, who's much taller and has boxed on a few of my shows. They'd planned to fight each other quite a long way in advance. I didn't to make the match, they did it themselves. That happens sometimes. Good mates in boxing before, good mates afterwards. Damian just edged the fight, because of his reach advantage, but Ricky - ever the entertainer - did a bit of showboating in the final round to get the crowd going.

The future

Two days after the event, everyone in the Facebook groups were planning the next ones. They want everything to be even bigger and better next time, to raise more money for a charity. Everyone working together to achieve something mega. That's what I want to do. I used to want more than anything to win the next belt, to get that world title. There's still not a day that goes by that I don't think of what could have happened if I'd not picked up those injuries. I'd have loved to be Ross the Boss, champion of the world. I had the talent, the power, the speed and the sheer determination to make myself world champion. Sadly, my shoulder didn't let me.

I'd never have thought I'd find myself saying this, because I thought nothing could ever replace the buzz I got from fighting, but I got that same buzz the last time I put on my white-collar show. When I retired, was that my story coming to an end?

No, it was the beginning of a hundred new stories.

Chapter 25

HOUSE OF CARDS

"For what is man, what has he got?
If not himself, then he has naught,
To say the things he truly feels,
And not the words of one who kneels,
The record shows I took the blows,
And did it my way"
Frank Sinatra (My Way)

I thought the previous chapter was going to be the end of the book. I wanted to end it on a high, talking about the show that I'd put on and where my life is headed now. My life's never that simple. There's never an ending. Something else always happens. In September last year (2018) my sister's fiancee 'Brows' was going off to Albufeira in Portugal for his stag do. I was at the pub to see them all off, when they suggested I should hop on a plane and join them. The next day I got a flight out there.

Things hadn't been going too well with Nicola for a while, just that in many ways we weren't quite seeing eye-to-eye on things. We'd been arguing a lot over recent months, and I was feeling like I had to tread on eggshells all the time. Maybe she felt the same, I don't know. Any argument we'd had for the past couple of years, she'd talk about 'splitting up' but I always chose to mend it, not end it. The night I landed in Portugal, I'd had a few too many to drink in the airport and on the plane. I carried on drinking with the lads in different bars. I got into a scuffle apparently - I can't even remember the scuffle. I do remember waking up in hospital. I'd either been stabbed or slashed. The lads thought I must have fallen on some glass, but the nurse at the hospital told me I'd been stabbed. It was just to the left of my ribcage. Nothing serious, but it could have been.

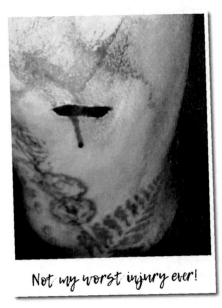

Not my worst injury ever!

When the nurse told me I had to sign some paperwork, I got a bit worried because I didn't know what had happened. I didn't know who'd done it, or why, so the last thing I wanted was Portuguese police. I shit mi'sen. We assumed it might have been one of the bouncers, because of where it happened. The nurse turned to the other bed, and I did a runner.

Luckily Jake-o and the lads had sent me a picture of the hotel that I was crashing in, because I'd not even made it that far the night before. I had just 3% battery on my phone, so I phoned Nicola and put it on charge. I didn't want her worrying, I was okay, so I didn't tell her about being stabbed.

The last thing I wanted was for her to be in a panic whilst I was in a different country. I left my phone on charge and headed out for some more drinks with the Valley boys. It was a stag do after all; what else were we going to do but drink?

About 7pm, Jake-o shouted me over. He had a message from Nicola on his phone. I'd been Dear-Johned. She was telling me she didn't want me any more and wanted a divorce.

I thought 'I could have not woke up this morning'; life's too short. I did call her a few times. I spoke to a few of the lads, and they said I'd changed over the years. Maybe it was the alcohol talking, but they said I needed to find myself again. I knew that the moment I got home, it would be a make-or-break moment with Nicola.

We stayed out drinking. They were celebrating Brows getting ready to be married; to me it didn't feel like that. To me it was drowning my sorrows, and I just kept drinking. I was pretty much out of it by the time we got back to the hotel, but at least this time I did make it back to the hotel...

I didn't make it back to the right room though. As I'd travelled at the last minute, I didn't have a room of my own and had to sleep on the sofa. I was drunk enough that I ended up crashing in the wrong room, with the lads who were staying for an extra day. The lads who were on the same flight as me woke up in the morning, saw I wasn't there, but didn't know that I was in the room next door. They didn't know where to find me, and of course I wasn't answering my phone.

They had to head off to the airport without me. By the time I woke up, it was too late. I woke up literally 40 minutes before the flight left. There was no way I could possibly make it in time.

Trying to patch things up with Nicola wasn't going to be easy after the night before anyway. After missing my flight as well? It was the final nail in the coffin.

The atmosphere was different; I just knew this time that it wasn't the same. They say that if you build a house of cards and knock the bottom one out, the whole house comes crashing down from removing just one card.

Don't get me wrong, I always try my best to still get on great with Nicola but the house of cards just comes crashing down once again. There's lots of things I want to be around for because of the boys. I don't want to turn to hating anyone just because we've split up. It's one of these things that can happen in life when you're headed in different directions.

For a while after that, I didn't know how to process things.

I started going out pretty much every night, partying and burning the candle at both ends. Suddenly, my life didn't fit with a nice, easy story to write as my autobiography. This book means something to me in a way; it's the story of me. You must know by now that I love myself a little too much. If you don't love yourself, who else is gonna love you? That's what I always say.

It got me thinking about my story, my legacy. You can't process all of that overnight, and sometimes I've felt that by going out partying, I could just get the little bit of space to distract myself. Living on my own, going out every night, was just like the old days - but better because I'm retired now. I'm limitless. My mates started to call me Rockstar Ross.

I'm pretty sure I must have undiagnosed ADHD. All my mates, anyone who's known me for more than five minutes, tells me that.

I started thinking about this book, wondering whether to go back and edit all the nice stuff that I'd said about Nicola. But why should I do that? That's how I felt about her; it's all true. I didn't want to change a single word about Nicola. It is what it is.

I have gone back and added in a few more stories though. Whilst I was with Nicola, out of respect for her, I didn't want to say too much about previous relationships. I feel like I can be a bit more free, a bit more open now, to talk about what's happened. I couldn't have talked about Becky or Lucy Victoria before, but those things are part of the story of my life. A lot of the things that happened explain why I am who I am today.

If you'd asked me a year ago, I'd have told you exactly what I thought the next chapter was going to hold for Ross Burkinshaw. I'd have been so wrong. Everything has changed.

I could tell you all about my latest Del Boy business ventures; I'm always doing something new, working alongside other people. I've got my own Ross The Boss branded boxing gloves. I'm working alongside Full Spectrum Oils selling CBD oils.

I could tell you about me and Claire, using my name for Boss Box Foods. We're doing a Boss Box Academy for mother and toddler groups, 'childrens' boot camps', and loads of other new ideas. I'm never short of ideas. Claire has ideas too, but she's also great at making sure I don't forget to put them into practice. There's always got to be something new for me. I have keep moving forwards. If you stand still, you're moving backwards.

Ross, Kelly & Martini

Today, I don't know exactly what the future holds. I've started a relationship with someone new, Kelly Wheeler, who's got a lot of the same interests as me - and who's a bit crazy like me. Alright, she's a *lot* crazy like me.

We got together through her brother, Blobby, who used to help me at my old gym in Pittsmoor years ago. He phoned me a few months back
to tell me that his sister was going to come up and train at the gym. I'd never met her before but she made a big impact; she doesn't shut the fuck up. We got talking straight away because there were only a couple of people at the session. We had a great laugh, but that's all it was at the time. The Saturday after I was at the Kettle Black. Kelly was out, playing gooseberry as her mate was with a lad.

She saw me and said "Oi, you! I want a word! I couldn't walk after that session."

I *think* she was on about the training. I mean, I *hope* she was on about the training - unless she was psychic and could see into the future...

Kelly said "I never wanted to go into a gym ever, but you made it enjoyable. I think I owe you a drink."

She bought me a Pornstar Martini. I said to the barman 'take a photo, I'll send it to your brother'. We had the picture, and instantly I thought we go together - so I worked reyt hard all week to take her out. Plus, I had to get permission from her brother.

In a short period of 11 weeks we've already been to Mexico together to my sister's wedding, and we've got lots of plans for the future. Writing this now, I certainly know where I want it to go.

I take each day as it comes. I don't have to know where it's headed. After meeting Kelly, I've started to slow down at least a little bit.

Ironically, we've put the finishing touches to this chapter the night before the book goes to press. It's April 23rd, 2019, St. George's Day; ten years to the day since I won my English title. A lot has happened in those ten years.

For Ross 'The Boss' Burkinshaw, life isn't just *any* rollercoaster. It's *my* rollercoaster and I ride it *my* way.